CLOAKED IN FAITH

Dearest Tina, thank you
for making my dreams
a reality
 " More unites us than
divides us; focus on the common
 humanity".

ROBERT G. LAWRIE

Warmest regards,
Rob

This book is a memoir. It reflects the author's present recollections of experiences over time. Some names and characteristics have been changed, some events have been compressed, and some dialogue has been recreated.

First paperback edition December 2018

ISBN 978-0-578-42153-7 (paperback)
ISBN 978-0-578-42488-0 (ebook)

Published by Robert G. Lawrie

Robert G. Lawrie is available to speak at your live event. For more information about booking an event or special discounts for bulk purchases, please contact the author at the website below:

www.roblawrieauthor.com

This book is dedicated to Fr. Thomas Zazella (Fr. Tom), who saved me with his love; to Maureen Powers-Smith, who shaped me with her love; to my children, Brett, Ethan and Erin who completed me with their love; and to the world with whom I endeavor to share love.

ACKNOWLEDGEMENTS

This book began as a handwritten testimony to the many trials and tribulations I have experienced throughout my life. Although many of the events were traumatic or negative in nature, they have been counteracted by the positive forces in my life. It is those positive forces that I want to acknowledge as they combined, have helped me endure, rise above, thrive and, most importantly, encourage others to rise above the negativity we all must encounter in life.

First and foremost, I must acknowledge the creator of all things. It is God whom I must thank for my life and all He has enabled me to accomplish within it. He has shaped me and brought me to this point in which I look to reflect His goodness and care for humanity. It is the steadfast faith I have in Him that enables me to travel through life with a positive outlook and hope for a better world. It is also through Him that I must thank the people He has placed in my life who have helped me as I travel along my journey.

Parents are typically the starting point and keystone for one's growth, stability and development of trust in others. Considering how the bond between me and my parents was broken at a very early age and the abusive environment in which I lived when I reunited with my biological father, my parents never were able to provide that foundation for me. Instead of a blood relationship, I received all those benefits from strangers who ultimately became my family.

My relationship with Father Tom spanned decades, and he would become the one I would regard as my true father. He taught me all of the necessary life skills, lessons and values I would rely on as I entered adulthood. He supported me, guided me and, most of all, loved me like a father should love a child. He showed me how an adult was supposed to be a role model and encourage a child to reach for the stars while planting firm roots. He helped me grow in spite of the lack of roots and wings which both my parents failed to give me. I have tried my best to emulate all of Father Tom's defining qualities, and as I grow older, I continue to strive to honor him.

My inclusion into the Smith family was a life-changing event as I would develop a close relationship with each member, especially with Maureen. I will always consider Maureen to be an angel sent by God as she helped shape me and prepare me for the world I was about to enter. She instilled in me the values and confidence I would need to help maneuver my life as I grew to become independent. She and her family showed me the love and support which a family is supposed to offer each other and through them I learned what a true family should be.

As I learned about family from the Smiths, I also need to thank my own children, Brett, Ethan and Erin. Having children of my own allowed me the advantage of seeing the world through others' eyes and the privilege of learning from them as much as having an impact on them. I can only hope they know how much of an inspirational force they are to me and how much of my heart they occupy.

Last but not least, I want to thank Cyndi Schulman. Her role as editor and business partner turned this book from a dream into reality. Her work ethic and adherence to self-imposed deadlines, outstanding writing and legal skills as well as her enthusiasm for expanding her experiences and perspectives were all instrumental in turning a handwritten manuscript into a finished published product. Beyond Cyndi's professional skills, her friendship and eternal optimism have been a constant source of support. She is a reminder that there are still people in this world who are honest, who are trustworthy, and who genuinely care for others. Her support for me and this project has been unwavering. She has walked steadfastly beside me and has helped transcend me from my lowest point to my highest, and for that, I am beyond grateful.

Transforming this original manuscript into *Cloaked in Faith,* has been a transformation for me as well. Despite difficult beginnings and challenging adult years, it has become increasingly clear to me that one's starting point does not have to be one's ending point. Through the combination of a goal, determination, faith, and love, all things are possible. Thank you to those who have shown me the love and support needed to achieve my goals and I, in turn, hope to do the same for others.

INTRODUCTION

Most people have never heard of Guyana. To those who may have heard the name, it is associated with the Jim Jones cult and drinking "Kool-Aid." For me, it goes much deeper than a little country next to Venezuela. It is a place of strong familial ties, a place that taught me which cultural values to accept or reject, and a place I am conflicted about calling home. Although I am fourth generation Guyanese, my broadened perspectives since immigrating as a teenager and becoming a US citizen have shown me that even though I cannot shed my heritage and lineage, I have learned that I must separate my past from my present and future and utilize only the positive forces from my past which have enabled me to advance.

Presently, I am an educator in a public school system and a PhD candidate in research methodology. My future includes plans to examine and analyze data reflecting many of society's issues which I have experienced firsthand. In understanding the causes and effects of many of these issues, policies and treatments can be instituted to remedy many of their consequences. If my past hardships can lead to future benefits, then there will have been a value to those experiences.

I came to this country at age fourteen with only my siblings and a suitcase. My American childhood ranged from living with an abusive father, to being on my own and homeless, to living in a rectory, and ultimately living with a foster family. Those very important formative years taught me much about life and the key to survival. Survival meant going to school and working a part-time job every day in order to pay for tuition. What little money was left went to cover necessities. Necessities, however, did not mean that I had everything I needed. There were plenty of days I did not have enough food or clothing to meet my needs. I relied on the generosity of a priest who mentored me, counseled me and cared for me to make up for what I lacked. Additionally, my emotional needs were not fully met. I had no family, no home address and no true friends—a terribly important component of the teenage years. Coming face to face with some very adult experiences at a young age, with no one to help me navigate those experiences, I was forced to learn some key life lessons on my own in order to cope and overcome. The lessons that I learned showed me that in spite of the existence of some ugly sides to life, there were ways to rise above it.

Fast forward to my adult years and the hardships and obstacles continued.

Over a span of thirty-five years I experienced unemployment, foreclosure, financial ruin, divorces, the loss of family and attempted suicides. The irony, however, is that despite these devastating events, I am in the best place now than I have ever been in my life. The incredible outlook I have on life all stems from the lessons I have learned and their application to my experiences.

I have written this book to share these life lessons and to help others overcome their own personal adversities. The experiences I share are real, though in the interest of privacy, the names of many of the people are not. Having endured these experiences has enabled me to create a strategy to not only survive negative forces, but to thrive. Through a combination of three forces, I am an example of how you can achieve whatever you want and can put yourself in whatever place in life you choose.

The first step is to design a goal or purpose for yourself. When I was at my lowest, losing the woman I loved and our children, I thought I had nothing left to live for. It was only through a reexamination of what is important to me that I was able to reestablish a purpose in my life which brought me out of despair. I now know without a doubt that my every focus is on helping others overcome their own adversities and it is that goal that gets me out of bed every morning. Because of the many mountains I have been faced with to climb, I have gained incredible perspective which gives me the foundation to be a support for others who are encountering their own hurdles. It was only through the establishment of this goal that I was able to pull myself up from the deepest depths. After all, how can you get anywhere if you don't know where you want to go?

The second force necessary, though no less important, is education. My being a first-generation college coed did not offer me the advantage of a support system to instruct me about the importance of learning. Nonetheless, I realized early on that education can raise you up to unimaginable heights. I have always held the highest regard for learning and I have seen from my own experience that knowledge and a degree give one options. Despite having all the cards being stacked against me: my immigrant experience, my lack of knowledge of American ways, my lack of basics, my lack of resources, and my minority status, I know education is the golden ticket to reach any goal one sets out for himself. It offered me my first opportunities after college and ultimately opened the door for me when I found my calling as an educator. It enabled me to reestablish my financial, social and emotional footing when I emigrated from the United States and returned penniless. Even now, as a PhD candidate, I know my degree, when it is ultimately received, will enable me to advance my purpose of helping others at a more significant level.

Finally, the last force necessary is that of sacrifice and hard work. In today's world, many believe that they are either entitled to certain benefits or rewards or that if they do not receive what they want, they give up. I adhere to the belief that if there is something you want, you work for it with no less than your all. My philosophy has always been that nothing will stop me from getting what it is that I want except for my own lack of effort. If you set a goal and seek it out, how can you expect to get it without effort? Of course, it may not materialize at first, but if the importance of it is still there, then so should the effort.

As you read this book and share my past experiences, it is my sincerest hope that the combination of forces that I have applied in getting beyond my obstacles helps show you a path to overcome your own personal adversities, whether similar to mine or not. No one can go through life without facing challenges or negative forces in one form or another. That is a reality. It is most important, however, to remember that one can always change his situation. Set a goal, work towards it and have faith. All things are possible.

SECTION I

GUYANA

CHAPTER 1

TIRA THE TERRIBLE

"I have an idea that the phrase 'weaker sex'
was coined by some woman to disarm the man she was
preparing to overwhelm."

- Ogden Nash

My grandfather Sydney Lawrie was the consummate philanderer, a behavior that was tacitly approved by my grandmother. Of course, one must consider the time and my grandfather's status when reflecting on this statement. Sydney's behavior frequently got him into a world of trouble not only with jealous husbands but also with potential suitors of the many women he pursued. I suppose in many ways this would explain my father's philandering habit as well. However, unlike my own parents, my grandparents fought battles together as a single unit. When adversaries would confront my frail grandfather, it was my grandmother, Tira, that ended up fighting on his behalf.

My grandfather started an affair, sanctioned by my grandmother, with one of the very young teen daughters that lived next door by the name of Toonks. My grandmother thought it was acceptable for a married man at that time and in that society to have a girlfriend, a concept no self-respecting woman would allow today. My mother, also in line with a modern woman's perspective, was no different as she was never too comfortable with the girlfriend concept and would share her dismay with her mother-in-law. Tira would promptly remind my mother that a man must have a "ghalfriend," married or not. Sydney and Tira saw eye to eye on this topic and my grandfather continued to have a good old time with Toonks as long as he kept giving her a "small piece," a little bit of money.

Over the course of time, Toonks developed a side relationship with a gentleman from the Pomeroon region of Guyana named Jeff. He was much younger than my grandfather and Sydney would have none of it. He started to make life miserable for Toonks and worst of all began to withhold the "small piece." In response to Sydney's continued harassment of Toonks, Jeff rose to the occasion to defend his lady's honor. On one of the many beautiful sunlit Guyanese afternoons, Jeff chose to confront my grandfather, at his house, in his village, while his wife, my grandmother, was home. This was a very poor decision, putting the suitor's physical well-being in mortal danger and his manhood into serious jeopardy. Jeff had already downed several drinks to work up the courage to confront my grandfather about his indiscretions. He came down the lone public road and stood in front of my grandfather's house and proceeded to espouse the values of Toonks and the lack of values on my grandfather's part in not so subtle tone or words.

"You fuckin' old cunt…Why don't you leave my woman alone? Why don't you stick with that old whore you have? You can't even perform, yet you're running after young women."

To which my grandfather kept interrupting, "You old Potagee rass, go back to Pomeroon…"

Jeff continued, "Just because your name is Lawrie don't mean you own anybody.

"Why don't you take your ass back to Pomeroon before I get Tira on you?" rebuked Sydney.

Jeff was either a very brave man or a very stupid one, and the ensuing actions towards Jeff by my grandmother in the next few hours would bear witness that the former option was not the case.

As Jeff continued to "buse," cuss, at my grandfather and with my grandfather's doing his best to persuade Jeff to go on about his business, my grandmother began the necessary preparations to handle the confrontation differently. She knew that if my grandfather's slanted rhetoric proved not to be persuasive enough to have Jeff desist from this life-threatening behavior, she would need to take matters into her own hands. Jeff should have known that my grandmother had quite an established and well-deserved reputation from the years of village warfare she had engaged in on behalf of my grandfather's arrogant ways. He was the brains and she was the muscle. Jeff was not one to be easily dissuaded from his defense of his lady by sound logic. For reasons unknown to the average person, after earnest pleadings from my grandfather to halt the actions in which he was engaged, Jeff chose to continue his assault.

As I had seen my grandmother do on numerous occasions, she began the preparations for battle. With a calm demeanor, a skill honed through the many battles she had fought on her own in her home village of Darthmouth and later on in defense of my grandfather in their current village of Better Hope, she made her way into her room. There I watched as she went through her pre-battle preparations. I was her favorite grandchild and therefore permitted to observe what could only be described as a teachable moment for her young grandson. My grandmother first methodically removed her dentures, a safeguard in the event of a frontal attack to her face. She placed them in a glass with water she kept for that purpose. Next, she removed the all-important wig that covered the two onion-size buns she had wrapped on the top of her head. The first phase of battle preparations was complete.

All the while Jeff continued to express his disregard for my grandfather's behavior toward his paramour. Sydney was becoming terribly worried at this point because he had seen my grandmother quietly leave his side from the veranda and knew what would be coming next. My grandfather was quite familiar with her battle preparations by this point and he knew that Jeff was really pushing the safe boundaries. He continued to extoll Jeff to leave as my grandmother moved into the second phase of battle preparedness.

Once the wig was removed and a red handkerchief was firmly tied around her head she proceeded to make her way down to the bottom of the house, which in Guyana was built on stilts in anticipation of the yearly coastal flooding. My grandmother made her way to the barn and got herself a nice strong rope "to bind she belly," to strap up her midsection which at this point had borne my grandfather 13 children. This undoubtedly had something to do with restricting all unnecessary moving parts during the heat of battle. She was almost ready for the assault except for the coconut oil which would be abundantly applied to her forehead and hands as an intimidation factor. The bright Guyana tropical sun against that terrorizing forehead, coconut oil shimmering at the zenith of same, would strike fear into the bravest of sober hearts, but not so with Jeff. In his zeal to protect his lady, Jeff was pushing the barriers of rational thought. Toonks' beau was about to become sober in a short minute and he didn't know it yet. Had he known what was coming, it would have defied logic to not try with every ounce of energy to vacate the premises in as brief an amount of time as possible. Alas, such was not the case of a disrespected suitor under the influence of spirits.

The coconut oil which my grandmother applied to her person also had two other practical uses. First, should her opponent get his hands on her, they would quickly slip off. Second, the oil would prevent cutting when she would deliver her most feared maneuver, the head butt. From where I stood at that moment, I knew this was going to be an especially bad confrontation, one to long be remembered in the annals of Lawrie family history. I was not to be disappointed.

The final step in the preparation for battle by my grandmother involved the physical transformation of my grandmother's demeanor. To this day I am still amazed at the startling change in my grandmother's face which went, in a few short seconds, from kind, loving, and angelic to totally demonic. I was terrified to see her in battle mode and cowered behind her as she began the long walk across the battlefield of my grandfather's front yard to confront the enemy. My cousin Amanda who enjoyed no other activity more than this, promptly fell in line behind me, her evil grin blossoming in anticipation of the spectacle about to unfold. Events upstairs on the veranda at this point had progressed to where my grandfather had just about given up in trying to persuade Jeff to leave. Anticipating the ensuing events, my grandfather proceeded to pull his rocking chair forward to get a better view of the action that would unfold in the next few minutes. Sadly, Jeff was about to find out in the most brutal and humiliating of events, the error of his ways. My grandmother, Tira the Terrible, was on the loose and she was angry, very angry.

Jeff, under the influence of alcohol stood no chance in the blistering attack which was about to strike him. My grandmother, due to her age, could not run to catch Jeff. And Jeff, being a man of Guyanese culture, would never run from a woman if being chased. A man's ego is cause for many a cardinal mistake, and Jeff's would cause him to pay a terrible price once my grandmother arrived. As Tira approached Jeff and he saw up close her demonic face, his cowardice emerged which then directed him to begin to walk away from my grandparents' home. However, by now, this was not an acceptable course of action for Tira the Terrible. She had gotten all dressed up to fight, and a fight she would have. Jeff continued to slink down the public road at a pace that was easily matched by my grandmother, and she was gaining on him steadily. Jeff's choices were few. He could run, but that would put him in a bad light to the local villagers and that was something he knew culturally was totally unacceptable. Instead, he opted for the alternative, which was to let my grandmother catch him, an equally terrible choice by any measure.

Jeff was a rather lean and frail looking fellow. My grandmother's first move once she was within hand's reach was to engage in the first rule of inside fighting. She narrowed the distance between them and took a firm grasp of his shirt. Once that vice grip was applied, Jeff was done. I remember the next act as vividly as if it happened yesterday. In a maneuver my father once used on me, (a skill he probably learned from my grandmother, with equally vicious results) my grandmother delivered her signature blow. She reared back about a good arm's length, and with a lightning strike characteristic of an enraged bull, delivered a butt using the side of her head. The impact was with such force that it ripped Jeff clean from her grip and laid him out flat like a sack of potatoes on the red loom of the Better Hope public road. Jeff rolled over a few times and scrambled to his feet, at which point he became fully aware of his extreme miscalculation. However, he was too late to stop it, and my grandmother was not finished. With poor Jeff still groggy from the vicious head butt, my grandmother came up to repeat the assault. It was a thing of beauty to behold and executed to perfection. She had come in low, up and under Jeff's chin and delivered a wicked slam. The hit caused Jeff to spin to the right, lose his balance, and fall into the drainage ditch that ran alongside the public road. Tira the Terrible was now going to finish the job. She lowered her body to prepare for the final blow. As she swooped down to launch herself towards the embankment, she delivered a third head butt to the soft tissue of Jeff's nose. It was a vicious and savage blow. Jeff flipped over in the water on his back and lay still, his eyes closed. He had been knocked unconscious by the third wave.

Tira the Terrible stood over Jeff's motionless body and began to compose herself. Slowly, she transformed back into the loving grandmother I knew. When she turned to walk back, she realized that the entire village had come out to witness the event. In this sleepy farming town, it was not often that one was treated to such an entertaining spectacle for all to see. The villagers pulled Jeff from the water and assisted him in order that he regain consciousness. The "cutass," the term commonly used to describe a proper "beatdown," would be remembered and heralded in the village lore even long after my grandmother's passing.

This, however, was not the end of the story. My grandmother had delivered such a complete and total victory over Jeff that she felt sorry for him as she saw him flat on his back on the public road. Jeff was laid out limp like a rag doll. He was wet, bloody, head and chin split open, and his clothes torn. My grandfather by then had made his way to the scene of the battle and as was customary of him, when the fighting was done, congratulated the victor on her efforts on his behalf. After the spectacle was complete and Jeff had regained consciousness, Sydney brought poor Jeff back to the house to be nursed to health. My grandmother, once cleaned up and re-fanged, proceeded to wash and sew up Jeff's torn shirt and to make him a nice dinner of hot bread and butter with fried eggs along with a cup of hot chocolate malt with fresh cow's milk. She then put him on the last bus to Charity, the neighboring village.

After that event there was not much dissent from Toonks about the status of their relationship. As the saying goes, "to the winner goes the spoils," and my grandfather took great pleasure in enjoying the spoils. Sydney, the victor by way of my grandmother, went back to his usual status with Toonks and all was well in the Lawrie household again. Needless to say, no one in Better Hope ever saw Jeff again. The last anyone heard about him was that he relocated shortly after that fateful day to

Venezuela where he was raising free range chickens. Hopefully, for Jeff, it would be the start of many better choices.

CHAPTER 2

BEGINNINGS

"The happiest moments of my life have been the few which
I have passed at home in the bosom of my family."

- *Thomas Jefferson*

Tira the Terrible may have truly represented a more accurate reflection of Guyanese culture, but not of my family's status and position in society. I was born Robert Gerald Lawrie ("Gerry" to my friends) in the village of Charity, which is located in the Pomeroon region of Guyana. This region of land, the former British Guiana, had been under British control and colonized since the early nineteenth century. My paternal great-grandfather, John Campbell Lawrie, came to this country from Scotland, as an overseer during this colonial period. After the settlers returned to Scotland and England, my great-grandfather agreed to remain in Guyana. In exchange for his decision to stay, he was granted a sizable holding of land. The acreage was in the village still known as Better Hope. Better Hope is situated along the Essiquibo Coast. It is bounded by the Atlantic Ocean on the northeast, the Essiquibo River on the southeast and the Pomeroon River on the west.

John Campbell Lawrie had three sons and two daughters from his first wife, a woman of East Indian descent. Sookdai, as she was known, had most likely come to Guyana as an indentured servant. My great-grandfather's wealth and the fact that he was of Anglo blood made the Lawrie family among the most respected in the region.

My grandfather, Sydney, was John Campbell Lawrie's second to last child with Sookdai. Sydney Lawrie inherited a significant portion of my great-grandfather's estate. He was a rice farmer, as were most of the land owners in that region at that time and was admired and well-regarded. Sydney did something that was unheard of in those days: he married a woman of African descent. My grandmother, the aforementioned Tira the Terrible, was not a woman to cross and was fiercely protective of her husband and her family. Tira was the true matriarch of the Lawrie clan. She and Sydney sired fourteen children, not including the three additional children Sydney fathered outside of the marriage. My father, Robert Reginald Lawrie, was the fifth child of my grandparents' fruitful marriage.

My father, like his father and grandfather before him, married someone of a different heritage. My mother, Winifred Brock, was the second child of three siblings, born from a dearth poor Amerindian woman from the Arawak tribe. My maternal grandmother came from the Amerindian region of Guyana known as Wakapoe. Although very poor, she was an immensely proud woman who believed in the value of education and passed that value system on to her daughters. My grandmother struggled mightily to raise my mother and her siblings, earning a meager "salary" by rowing a handmade canoe for a midwife to earn a living. Yet she, like my paternal grandmother, made certain her children would be cared for and educated, enough so that my mother was able to elevate herself to the position of principal of the local school.

I, therefore, became the true melting pot. When one looks at me, my heritage is indistinguishable. I suppose I racially represent what the world may look like as it heads to becoming a more unified global community. I carry five races in me with

Native American being the dominant one. During colonial times, Guyana was a deeply racist and segregated society. In many ways it remains the same today. People tended to live in villages determined by their race. One could call it voluntary segregation. On the Essequibo Coast where I lived, there were three predominately Afro-Guyanese villages: Darthmouth, from where my grandmother originated, Danielstown and Queenstown. The remaining villages were predominately Indian except for my village of Better Hope, where the entire Lawrie clan lived. We were a mixture of white, black, East Indian and, in the case of my mother, sisters and me, Amerindian. Every race basically kept to themselves, but when it was harvest time, my grandfather would hire laborers from all different lineages to work on the estate.

I interacted with everyone without regard to ancestry not fully comprehending the effects of the segregated nature of Guyanese culture. As a young boy growing up in Guyana, I hated being from a mixed racial background. I would have much preferred to be a member of one race—any race. Like most children, I wanted to be like everyone else that surrounded me, either black or Indian. Being multiracial evoked disparaging remarks from others and caused me to always feel like an outsider. I never fit in with any group. I was called "buck" (a derogatory term equivalent to the "N" word) so many times that I thought it was my name. I disliked the term but did not realize that I may have been a target of racism. Ironically, after living for decades in the United States, I would return to Guyana to marry my wife, only to hear the term being used by my wife's family to describe Amerindians of whose blood ran through my veins and the veins of my children.

Even Tira did her utmost to limit the features in us that showed our race. As a child, I did not realize her intentions to mask any of our features which would identify us as having color. Sadly, I have experienced first-hand people who resent their black identity. I believe so many negative stigmas and stereotypes have been perpetuated on the black race that many people of color start to affirm them and come to despise their own color. Even today, in my own classroom, many black students find excuses not to admit to their race. It is even worse when people of color make other people of color feel inadequate about their own race. I have experienced students who come to me and ask why their classmates make fun of them for speaking correctly and carrying themselves in a certain way that is associated with the white race. What does one say to a student under those circumstances? Racism cuts very deep and as I have learned and experienced more in my years in America, I have come to detest this aspect of society with unadulterated passion.

As I have aged, I have learned to appreciate my mixed heritage and while I am disheartened by the animosity and outright hatred that racial groups display towards one another, I am hopeful that I can use my multi-ethnicity to bridge these divides. Being a part of many different groups offers me the advantage of exposing others who are of single races to the perspectives and ways of other varying cultures. I am extremely vocal in sharing my opinions on racism and encourage all people to be open to all others. I believe in the basic goodness of human beings and will forever strive to live a life that transcends race, ethnicity, gender, poverty, class and any other divisive factor that often prevents us from becoming whomever God intended.

A few years after my birth, my parents moved back from Charity to Better Hope where the large bulk of the Lawrie clan resided. My earliest memories are from my days in Better Hope. I lived in what was referred to as a "privilege home" in that it was new, well-maintained and painted. The house rested on the ocean side of the only public road that traversed the coast of that region of Guyana. My home was built with wood, painted white, with a red zinc roof and blue trim around the glass louvered windows. There was a porch located in both the front and the rear. The structure was built on stilts, like all homes along the Essiquibo Coast, to protect it from the constant tidal surges. Out back was a yard and the outhouse. Beyond the yard, there was a canal which ran parallel with the coast. This served as yet another buffer to help protect the homes and crops from being overrun by the salty Atlantic waters. The house itself was small—just four rooms. There was a gathering room, a kitchen, a bedroom for my parents and a bedroom to be shared by my three sisters and me. Across the public road was where hundreds upon hundreds of acres of rice crops lay to be harvested by our family.

These days of my early childhood in Guyana were among the happiest days of my life. My mother was a physically beautiful woman who valued learning and became a respected citizen in the community. She became an effective and respected educator, a difficult feat due to the societal limitations of her Amerindian ancestry. My father, a handsome and machismo man and the favorite of Sydney, commanded great respect and admiration from the villagers. My parents appeared from the outside to be the ideal couple. Together with my three sisters and me, we were the perfect Guyanese family. They provided us many happy memories during these very early years. Birthdays were special around the house and my mother would insist on having parties with all our friends there to help celebrate. Mom would always insist that we employ all the good manners that had been passed down through the generations of the Lawrie family. My mother, notwithstanding her exceedingly humble beginnings was a classy and proud woman and understood the value of manners. She went to great lengths to ensure that these behaviors were ingrained into our very core. She demanded only the best of etiquette from my sisters and me. It was considered high class to have such manners and my mother insisted that the Lawrie family was of high class.

It was on one such birthday that I received my little green tricycle, my most favorite of my childhood toys. On the back of the tricycle was a place where a friend could ride with me. I would ride with my little sister, or my friend Azra or even one of my numerous cousins who lived along the public road. I learned to ride and to play with an unlimited imagination. I would ride shirtless wherever my tricycle would take me, immune from the summer sun, which would burn almost everyone else. Perhaps God had a purpose to protect me with my mixture of black, Anglo and Native American blood. I did not know and at that age, I did not care. Instead, I would turn copper each summer, earning the nickname "Copper Color." Sydney and Tira's house was two lots away, separated from our house only by a vacant lot where my parents would cultivate beans. Almost daily, I would hop on that tricycle and ride to and from my grandparents' house, my hair turning red from the intense summer sun.

Memories of meals and bath time stand out to me from those early years. Tira was a phenomenal cook, having ample opportunity to hone her culinary skills with a spouse and 14 children. Her recipes included the likes of "cook-up," a rice and beans mixture with any type of fish or meat, "methegy," a mixture of boiled ground provisions in coconut milk and mixed with ham or beef, "roti" or "dholl," a hard baked dough with hot imported British margarine, and my personal favorite, "gula-gula," a dough made with flour, milk and sugar and flavored with raisins and cinnamon. The gula-gula would be prepared in a deep pan known as a "canari," and fried in coconut oil until golden brown. Being the favorite of my grandmother, I would always receive the largest portion. Before devouring these treats, I would inhale the aroma while they were still hot and fresh. Those deep breaths often resulted in sweat flowing down my forehead due to the mixture of the heat of the day and the temperature of the food.

Bath time was a family affair. Tira would send me and my countless cousins, all of whom were my best friends, to bathe in the canal behind our house. The canal served many purposes. Not only were fish and shrimp caught there, but the water was also used for bathing and washing clothes. On occasion it served as a local toilet for some of our neighbors, a practice which was strictly forbidden by my mother. Bath time could last an hour, with games being the bulk of the time spent in the water. We would then proceed indoors where we were greeted with the ritual of being fully moisturized in coconut oil. According to Tira, the coconut oil was a moisturizer and a cure-all for any ailment. She would use it as well to paste down the hair on my head, so that it would stay straight and not show the curls from my African ancestry. I can remember how the oil would come running down my face. Tira understood the stigma attached to her race and did everything in her power to cover or hide those features in us. Even though I knew my grandfather was deeply in love with her, Tira knew that she reminded him daily of her African ancestry. She would do what she could to make our lives less subject to any bigoted influences. If the coconut oil could cure racism, well then, by all means, she was going to give it a try. Oddly enough, Tira also claimed that the coconut oil served as a particular male teenage right-of-passage whereby one would be cleansed in coconut oil using a "nenwha" scrub (a dried local plant) for the purpose of protecting teenage boys from all manipulative powers of a woman. In retrospect, as much as I adored my grandmother, I should not have relied solely on the powers of the coconut oil when it came to women. Another lesson I have since learned.

CHAPTER 3

NO MORE ROSE-COLORED GLASSES

"I'm not crying because of you; you're not worth it.
I'm crying because my delusion of who you were was
shattered by the truth of who you are."

- Dr. Steve Maraboli

B eing a young child offered me the priceless gift of
acceptance through naiveté which enabled me to be happy
without understanding my true reality. I was under the age of
five and, therefore, mostly unaware of a lot of the blossoming
dysfunction in my family. Sure, there were the occasional
arguments and fights with no shortage of screaming, or
"bussing" as it was commonly called. My mother and Tira were
frequently at odds, which I later determined was due to my
father's lack of attention to matters at home. It was not,
however, until the event with my Uncle Harold occurred that I
began to get a window into reality and learned how family
dysfunction could lead to heartbreak, something that would be
repeated in an endless cycle over the course of my life.

Uncle Harold, my father's brother, was mean and brutish.
He physically and emotionally abused my mother, my siblings
and me. Over the years I had watched him slap my mother over
a few vinyl records she had lent him which he did not want to

return. He slapped her so hard she nearly broke her neck falling down the steps of my grandparents' home. This was the same Uncle Harold who tried to cut another brother's head off with a machete because he wasn't invited to a party that my grandparents hosted. That uncle who received the wicked chop from the machete-wielding Uncle Harold suffered the loss of a finger and an injury to the hand he had held up trying to stave off the impending blow. Uncle Harold was Tira's favorite child and he would favor Tira in the dust-ups between my mother and grandmother. For some bizarre reason, Harold believed that he could show his favor toward Tira by being cruel to my mother and me. One day, when Harold saw my little green tricycle parked in front of my grandparents' home, he seized upon the opportunity to inflict his form of cruelty by driving his tractor over and flattening my tricycle, rendering it unsalvageable. I was devastated as my prize possession was obliterated. Most significantly, I learned for the first time in my life two very important realities. One: that loved ones, or those considered to be loved ones, can truly cause hurt more than I could ever have imagined; and, two: that over time, pain will eventually heal. I learned these two realities at a very early age and I would learn them again and again over the course of my life. In later years, Uncle Harold would force us out of our home, taking the house that my grandfather had given to my mother to hold for me as my inheritance. I still have the now useless documentation that evidences his wishes that I should inherit that home, despite Uncle Harold's confiscation.

Shortly thereafter, my father decided to immigrate alone to the United States, following his older brother Charles, in search of the American Dream. My father left my mother, three sisters and me with nothing but hope and a prayer. It was the first step in the shattering of a family that would never again be the same. Within months of my father's departure, my mother joined him to actively pursue the same dream as he, leaving my siblings and me behind. I was told the plan was to bring the four of us to the United States where we could all be a family together. But as often in my life, that plan never came to fruition.

My eldest sister Joan, who was about eleven at this time, became the surrogate mother of our family and she adjusted seamlessly to the role. She learned to cook, bake bread, grocery shop, iron our clothes and, what I believe was her favorite part of motherhood, administer discipline. She would whip us worse than mom, a total tyrant in all regards. Joan was a proud child for as long as I can remember, and she was my favorite sister as well as being the favorite child of my father. When she was young, both she and my father shared a hatred of their black ancestry. My siblings and I are all twenty-five percent black but somehow this mixing of races was unacceptable in her view. She felt trapped in her own body and felt shame. It would not be until later in her life, when she would serve in the United States Air Force, where she interacted with many people of color, that she matured and learned to embrace her lineage. By accepting and taking pride in her own blended heritage, she ultimately learned to love and respect individuals of all colors. Joan is living proof that people can change, and racism can be abated.

Marcy, the middle of my three sisters, physically displayed our African lineage more than the rest of us. Her personality was most like Tira the Terrible. On numerous occasions, Marcy would bail me out of the jams I had created for myself. I had developed an absolute lack of respect for others which frequently resulted in my being beaten by the neighborhood boys. However, Marcy would always seem to be there for me, exacting revenge upon my aggressors. She possessed a warrior's mentality and was ready to fight anyone, male or female, to protect someone she loved. It is a strength she still holds today even as her body ages and has physically broken down as she battles with poor hearing and weakened knees.

My youngest sister, Sharon, was the prettiest as well as the smartest of all of us. She was my little sister and I cared deeply for her. She was a fragile little girl with curly blonde hair and as cute as a button. I wept the most for her on the day I would eventually immigrate to the United States, leaving her behind. It would be another fourteen years until I would see her again. By that time, she was an adult with a child of her own. To this day, I am saddened to think of the lost childhood sibling relationship I might have had with her.

My mother and father took a one-bedroom apartment in a tenement building in Brooklyn, New York. Mom got a job working in a factory and my father worked as an orderly at a hospital. It was a manual labor job, one that he always felt was beneath him. My mother would remind him of this whenever he got caught up in his lies. With my father's frequent womanizing, his lying happened repeatedly, and they apparently often ended up in fights. My controlling father required that his uniform be ironed and starched daily by my mother. Should she fail to do so, the result was either a cussing out or a beating, or worse, being locked out of the apartment in the winter months without a coat. Years later I would recall her talking about the hard times they spent in Brooklyn. She had discovered, as all poor immigrants did, the hardships of making a new life in pursuit of the American Dream.

While my mother and father struggled in the United States to make a better life for us, I was enjoying my youth to the utmost. Joan's wrath aside, there was no true strong disciplinarian in the household. At school I proceeded to take my mischievous acts to new heights. I would throw bricks at passing cars. I swam in the prized tilapia farm pond at school. I ate what I wanted to eat and went where I wanted to go. I was not concerned with rules as I believed they did not apply to me. I was a bully. My mother had been a principal at the school I attended, and I felt this entitled me to special privileges.

I teased little girls, picked fights with older boys, raided neighborhood fruit trees and was the proud owner of one of the ugliest, filthiest vocabularies a little boy could possess. I feared nothing and while picking fights with the older boys, I would usually end up on the wrong side of the beatings. These experiences, however, would prepare me for later in life in the hardcore urban areas of Newark and Paterson, New Jersey.

While these acts of self-destruction are not so rare in young boys with little parental oversight, one such escapade of mine nearly resulted in the death of my entire family. One of the well-to-do families in my village owned a fishing boat and employed a local guy by the name of Jango to be a sailor on their vessel. Jango was widely feared and his reputation for evil, immoral and cruel acts was well-known by all, especially after visits to the local rum shop.

Jango's routine included going down to the local liquor shop and imbibing until he was uncontrollably drunk. Subsequent to his drinking bouts, he would oftentimes stop by my grandmother's house, steal some chickens, and cook them up to satisfy his drunken hunger. These were the same chickens which I was responsible for raising behind our house and the same chickens which provided a significant source of our sustenance in our struggle to survive. Thus, Jango's drunken habits were a source of great irritation to me. One afternoon, feeling especially mischievous, I stood at our window and proceeded to tell Jango, in quite colorful language, what I thought of his menacing ways. I bussed him over and over about the chickens he stole and about his drunken ways.

Well it must have been that Jango's afternoon drinking was especially heavy that day and at about half past nine that evening Jango decided to pay our house a visit. The weather was ugly. There was a late-night squall coming in off the Atlantic Coast, just a few hundred feet from our home. We had no streetlights or even electricity. It was pitch black outside and the rain lashed against the glass window panes and pelted against the zinc roof over our house. Lightning flashed in intervals of what seemed to be two to three minutes followed almost immediately by the deafening roar of thunder. Out from this storm came a most agitated, determined, and severely crazed Jango. He was a drunken man on a mission to correct the tongue lashing which I had inflicted upon him earlier that day.

The banging on the heavy wooden door in the front of our home awakened me and everyone else in the house. The door rested at the top of the staircase which led from the outside of the house. Next to the door along the length of the front porch, ran glass windows and when Jango could not break down the door, he moved on to break in through the windows. We were all watching Jango, standing at the window, an evil sneer on his face and a hunting knife in his hand, staring back at us as the lightning flashed behind him.

My grandmother told us to start yelling. We were instructed to scream so as to try and awaken the neighbors. But the sounds of the storm drowned out the screams and I saw certain death approaching. I believe my grandmother saw the same and she decided to run out the back in an attempt to draw him away from us. She would attempt to run, all sixty-eight years of brittle bones, the 600 yards across the field to my grandfather's home. Jango gave chase after her and caught up with her about halfway across the field. By then the storm had somewhat abated and we could hear her crying for help. Luckily, so did many of the neighbors in the village including my Uncle Ivan, who started out after Jango, chasing him into a nearby mangrove swamp.

They found my grandmother in some bushes a short while later. Apparently, my uncle had arrived in the nick of time to prevent a far worse scene. All that Jango had managed to do, beyond frightening us all, was to rip a few pubic hairs from my grandmother's body. Jango was subsequently located and brought up on charges. However, he would manage to pay off the officials and the case was dismissed. For Jango, he was a free man. For us, the damage was done. My grandmother had had enough after this life-threatening event. She wanted to return to the comfort of her own home in the village she knew so well, so she packed her belongings and left us alone as she returned back to Charity. My sisters and I were now forced to find our way and to survive in the best way we knew how.

CHAPTER 4

FOOTLOOSE

"How much more grievous are the consequences of anger
than the causes of it."

- Marcus Aurelius

Shortly after the Jango incident and my grandmother's departure, Joan wrote our mother in the United States and advised her of the circumstances in which we found ourselves. Alarmed, my mother decided to immediately return to Guyana. This decision had both positive and negative implications for me. Sure, it would be much better to live with a true adult as head of the family. However, while my mother was abroad, I had managed to become a total free spirit. I had sold off both pairs of my shoes, a valuable commodity at that time. I had allowed most of my clothes to become lost or torn. Almost half of my teeth had fallen out as a result of eating too much candy. My lack of personal hygiene had facilitated the accumulation of a half inch of dirt behind each of my ears. Worst of all, I had failed a grade in primary school. These were things I knew my mother would not take kindly to upon her return.

My mother arrived at our home to quite a disaster. She immediately set out to right the wrongs that took place in her absence. The most primary task, and certainly the most difficult for me, was the transfer of power from Joan back to my mother. In my mother's absence Joan had become quite deft at administering discipline in the form of beatings, her favorite part of being the substitute mom. The transition occurred in one rather quick simple move. My sister Marcy had started to misbehave, and Joan did what she had become accustomed to doing. She landed Marcy a right hook to her stomach which resulted in Marcy's wailing at the top of her lungs. When my mother asked Joan what had happened, Joan claimed she had "barely touched" Marcy. My mother responded by "barely touching" Joan, a touch that was delivered with such force that it immediately ceased all disciplinary measures on the part of Joan and ended her short authoritarian reign. Empress Joan had been stripped of her power in one quick act and, I must admit, I was not at all sorry for that.

I was not an easy child to raise and perhaps one can view events later in my life as some kind of punishment or response from God for my misbehavior. I would like to think, however, that I have more than paid for those bad deeds, and I do not believe that God is that vindictive. I was simply an incorrigible child and my mother's daily beatings could not shake me from my poor choices. No tree was left unclimbed. No neighbor's fruit trees were safe from daily raids. No lizard, bird, frog, caterpillar or spider in the vicinity of five square miles of my house had a day's rest or relaxation. Even those poor little sand crabs, which had been a food staple for my mother's family when she was growing up, were not safe. I would terrorize those crabs by tying a piece of thread around the claw of the creature and putting him next to his hole in the sand. The crab would naturally try to make a dash for the opening. As soon as he thought he was secure, I would drag him out by the piece of thread. This could go on for hours until, eventually, the poor creature would give up and release its claw or it would simply break off. I was so abusive, that both friends and strangers could not escape the venom of my filthy tongue. I had learned to cuss with the best of the drunken sailors, taught to me by the fisherman I hung around with when they brought in their daily catch to be sold on shore. These fishermen seemed to take a liking to me because I was ready to fight or do anything they requested at the drop of a hat. My poor mother did try to reform me, but it was to no avail. It would eventually take my living a life in America to do what my mother could not.

Another favorite pastime of mine over those long summer months was to go crabbing with friends. To have the optimal experience, we would look for crabs in the mangroves in the back of the village during the high tides of August. This time of year, when the moon was full, literally hundreds upon hundreds of crabs would come in on the tide. I consider these to be the best tasting crabs. I have eaten countless varieties, yet this "buck" crab, as it is known, ranks as the most delicious. Before heading out on one particular crabbing adventure, my buddies and I each got a "paddy" bag, the bags that were used to collect the freshly cut rice. As a boy I constantly tested faith and boundaries, regardless of whatever limits my mother may have imposed upon me. No matter how many times she whipped me, I simply crashed through her restrictions and did what I wanted. Going to catch crabs at high tide was one such boundary I totally disregarded. The crabs were out in abundance that day and most of the villagers were there, getting their fair share of the crabs. I was filling my bag, but not with the best quality of crabs. Because I was small and the tides were strong, the water kept tossing me back against the seawall with every wave. However, from where I was filling my bag at that moment, I could see a dead mangrove tree not too far off, and it was teeming with crabs. It had to be what I thought was a good six hundred feet from the shore, but I was certain I could make the swim. I tied my half-filled paddy bag around my waist. I was wearing only a pair of short pants, my skin golden brown from the Guyana sun. Although slight of frame, I was bold and determined. I paddled my way out to the dead tree that was being overwhelmed by some of the best-looking crabs of the season. Swimming against the lashing waves, I struggled across the gap. Halfway out, I knew I was in trouble. The distance to the tree was farther than I had anticipated, and the weight of the crab bag was pulling me under. I was sinking below the waves and as I was so small, I thought no one was going to see me. Desperate to stay alive but unable to untie the half-filled crab bag that was dragging me down, I took what I thought would be my last breath and disappeared below the surface. I flailed my last desperate kicks to try to stay afloat in a quest to survive. As I slipped below the waves, I felt a hand grab me around my neck and start to pull me above the water and back toward the shore. Someone had arrived in just the nick of time to save my life. My limp body was dragged to shore and the villagers somehow managed to get the salt water out of me and get me back to a functional state. Needless to say, when I got home and my mother found out about the incident, as she always did, a proper "cutass" ensued. I later learned that my savior that day was our milkman, Scott. He was a former student of my mother's, who by the grace of God, simply happened to be nearby. That same Scott would end up catching me for my mother as I ran down the public road to get away from her when it was time for my customary beatings. I would run, and she would chase me. I believe in some twisted way that my mother enjoyed those frequent cutasses she inflicted on me. It would be a few years, but soon enough it would be my father who would inflict those same beatings on me.

Chapter 5

"The End of the Innocence"

"When 'happily ever after' fails
And we've been poisoned by these fairy tales
The lawyers dwell on small details
Since daddy had to fly"

- Don Henley

My mother had returned following the incident with Jango. My parents' plan was for my father to stay in the United States to build a foundation and then send for the rest of the family to unite together. Like many immigrants of that era, he had come to the United States illegally. He took a job assembling parts in a factory with many immigrants like himself, while he lived in a small studio in Brooklyn among a large West Indian population. He eventually landed a better paying job as an orderly at a hospital, as mentioned earlier. He was not there very long before he met Dorothy Wright, who would later become my stepmother, a long-suffering but evil woman in her own right.

Dorothy, or Dot as she was most commonly known, was from a tiny island off the coast of Guyana called Wakenaam. She had trained as a nurse in Guyana and brought those skills to the United States which enabled her to have a relatively decent paying job as a nurse where my father worked. She, however, was a legal United States citizen. Marrying a citizen was one of the ways for an illegal immigrant to become a legal resident. Many United States citizens have earned quite a bit of money through so called "business marriages" as that kind of arrangement has benefits to both parties involved. For Dot and my father, those benefits were inescapably alluring.

Shortly after meeting Dot, and I am sure bedding her, my father wrote my mother, telling her that he had found a way to get his green card which would allow him to become a legal citizen. This arrangement would enable him to bring the family to the United States. My father, omitting the facts about the personal side of this new relationship, told my mother that he was going to enter into a business marriage. He explained that in order for him to proceed with the business marriage with Dot, he would first need a divorce from my mother. She agreed all the while believing that this was being done in the best interest of the family. The next time my mother saw my father after their divorce was finalized was about three years later. My father returned to Guyana at that time with his "business" wife and, to everyone's surprise, his new daughter in order to show them off. My poor mother was crushed. I still remember us looking through the cracks in the wall of our old dilapidated house at my stepmother and half-sister. We stared at the two women as he paraded them along the road of our village for all to see. My father betrayed the entire family to satisfy his own personal desires. Once again, I would learn the lesson of being hurt greatly by those we love. And once again, I would have to learn to allow that pain to heal.

My father has committed many despicable acts in his lifetime, but the one that will forever stay in my memory is what he pulled to divorce my mother. It would forever change my life and irreparably destroy the foundation of my beliefs about love and family. I know that the life of an immigrant to the United States is never easy. It is a choice which includes and centers around countless sacrifices. Those departing the country and those staying behind are often emotionally scarred for a lifetime. Such were the sacrifices made by my parents, perhaps more so by my mother than by my father. He just wanted to be free and move on with his life as he embraced better economic and social opportunities, never mind the carnage he left in his wake.

Life became more difficult following my parents' divorce. We were forced to constantly move as a result of my mother's being thrown out of my father's house and her trying desperately to support all of us as a single working mother. When my father saw fit, which was not very often, he would send a few dollars for the family. If we were lucky, he would send one hundred U.S. dollars, maybe once every three months in order to take care of four children. These were some of the most difficult days of our lives. My mother cried often. Walking home from school, her hand wrapped tightly around mine, she would tell me about my father. The stories seldom ended without her breaking down in tears. Her love for him endured even after many years beyond the divorce, even though he had long moved on and our life in Guyana was so difficult. We were four children living with a single mother who could not afford to support us. We were forced to move from place to place. There were times we relocated as many as seven times in a year, forever at the mercy of landlords, most of whom were extremely mean and nasty. It was rough on me because as soon as I made friends in one place, I had to pick up, move someplace else, and start all over. As difficult as this was on me, this constant moving was twice as rough on my mother and siblings, especially my proud sister Joan.

Money and necessities were scarce due not only to the reality of a single mother raising four children, but also due to the then current political climate. The Guyanese president at that time, Linden Forbes Samson Burnham, was experimenting with socialism. Basic commodities such as sugar, flour and rice could not be found in the stores. Although Guyana was a rice and sugar-producing nation, those items were not available for local consumption because those products were exported to get desperately needed foreign currency. Forbes Burnham's intentions to make Guyana self-sufficient were noble, but not practical for the Guyanese economy or people. It was a failed experiment. Many Guyanese suffered terribly under that regime. There was no food to be found in the stores, and when it could be found, one could not afford it. This was a time during which most went hungry. There was a weekly bread ration instituted every Saturday under which one small loaf of bread would be all an entire family would have for the week. Any additional food had to be home-grown as it was not available for purchase. People got by on one or two meals a day. I remember the rice which we were able to procure had worms in it. Although we were a rice-producing country, the best rice was saved for export. Flour was banned and expensive when it could be found on the black market. That too, when procured, had bugs in it. My mom would manage the best she could. I remember after she made bread in the morning with the bad flour, we had to spend five minutes taking the dead bugs and weevils out before we could eat it. Those bugs left a nasty taste in the bread. In my younger days we would have had butter to go with that bread, but in the Burnham days, we did not. Butter was also banned. Sugar, a favorite of mine, was also scarce. I remember running next door to my aunt's home to beg for some sugar. She was one of the most kind and generous people and so she would scrape from the bottom of her wet sugar jar to accommodate my plea. It was in wet clumps, but it satisfied my sweet tooth, a craving that would often send me to the dentist at a time when we certainly could not afford such a luxury. We did the best we could to survive in those days, and yes, life's focus was all about survival.

Over time, my mother grew more and more distant from my father and she began dating again. At one point my mother chose to date a man of African ancestry named John, which did not sit well with Joan. Joan did everything possible to make John's existence a living hell. He tried to win us all over by singing to us, taking us for rides in his luxury car and providing us with British imported chocolates. It never worked for Joan and since I followed her obediently, I was also not won over. As long as Joan was not happy with John for whatever reason, he would not find favor with me either. Although we would have liked to see my mother be happy, I suppose we never really got past the divorce and refused to accept another man in my mother's life. Marcy, on the other hand, who will make decisions based on what benefit it brings her, was all too happy to accept the chocolate treats even if it meant to accept John's involvement with our mother. She gladly accepted and wolfed down the chocolate in exchange for letting John have his way with mom. She is fond of saying that she would just as easily sell my behind for a few hundred dollars, or that she would pimp me out for a percentage of the profits. Sharon, my youngest sister, simply mimicked Marcy's actions. There was a definite rift between siblings as far as an approach to my mother's single life was concerned, as if we really should have any say in the way she conducted her life. Unfortunately, as events would have it, John died shortly thereafter in a horrible automobile accident and as sad as Joan was for my mother, she was happy their relationship had ended. When it was time for the funeral, mom prevented Joan and me from attending. Only Marcy and Sharon were permitted to accompany my mother.

My mother's actions as she re-entered the dating world caused us much stress. She engaged in a few relationships which caused us humiliation as well, including an illicit one with a former student. This caused residents of the village to further disrespect us. People would come to our home in the middle of the night and throw stones at the rusted zinc roof of our dilapidated house. It was a very rough time for us. My mother did what she needed to do to retain her sanity but as for Joan and me, we could not wait to somehow get away from it all.

SECTION II

NEW JERSEY

CHAPTER 6

"COMING TO AMERICA"

"...Home
Don't it seem so far away
Oh, we're traveling light today
In the eye of the storm
In the eye of the storm..."

- Neil Diamond

At some point in my father's life, his conscience got the better of him. He decided he wanted his previous family again, so he started, or shall I say Dot started to make preparations to bring us to the United States. Since my father was not a U.S. citizen and Dot was, it was up to her to initiate and follow up with all of the paperwork necessary to complete the process to allow us entry into the United States. Additionally, it was Dot's salary which was needed to help sponsor us to immigrate as my father's job was not financially sufficient. After several broken promises and much fanfare Joan, Marcy and I, accompanied by my grandmother Tira, managed to leave Guyana for the United States on June 18, 1978.

I believe Joan was the most excited to be leaving Guyana as she was not on the best of terms with my mother. As is customary when leaving the passenger waiting section in the airport, before walking out to the plane, one would turn and wave that final goodbye to family members. Joan, kept her head perfectly straight and walked directly onto that plane, not once turning back around. Little did she know that she would not visit Guyana again for over thirty years. I would not see my mother or Guyana for another eleven years. This type of separation, which is typical for many immigrant families more times than not, can often destroy the bonds of family. I know it did with mine.

I will never forget the flight from Guyana to the United States. I wore a pair of brown corduroy slacks and a blue and white plaid shirt. On my feet were a pair of tan hushpuppy shoes that were two sizes too small that squeezed my feet for the 5-hour flight to New York. Joan, temporarily reasserting her dictatorial ways, refused to let me take them off as she said my feet would smell. We landed at JFK airport in New York on a beautiful summer day late in the afternoon. Our seamless arrival gave us no indication of the experiences which would ensue and the life I would endure in the United States.

Life as an immigrant to America is never easy. Newcomers attempt to put down roots, but it can often feel like trying to plant those roots in rocky soil. So many things are strange and new to an immigrant which makes the dream for success very uncertain. The first difference I noticed upon my arrival was the houses. American homes are not built on the concrete or hardwood stilts that Guyanese homes are built upon to help protect them against the seasonal flooding. The basements of American homes were a new concept to me. The irony is that many immigrants start out in America living in very cramped quarters, oftentimes living in poorly insulated basements that are both illegal and fire traps. In fact, one of the first things many Guyanese immigrants will do is to try to buy a home and then rent out as many rooms of it as possible. The food is also unfamiliar. Guyanese staples are curry, rice and bread whereas pizza is an American favorite. Most significantly, however, the

American lifestyle differs dramatically from the Guyanese ways. In the United States, one has to constantly strive to do better in order to succeed. Either you work, or you remain at the bottom levels of society. The disparity of wealth between the United States and Guyana is a constant reminder to the poor immigrant of what he does not have, but what he can potentially attain if he makes the right moves on the chessboard of life in America. Sadly, one wrong move combined with a lack of determination and ambition can leave you with nothing but promises, regrets and broken dreams. This was the new world my sisters and I discovered upon entering America. It was truly a dog eat dog world.

After a forty-minute ride, we arrived at my father's house in Paterson, New Jersey. This would be my home for the next year and a half. It was a place characterized by emotional and physical abuse inflicted by both my father and stepmother that was beyond comprehension. Such abuse led to my sisters' being shipped off to the Air Force and my being relegated to the four walls of my father's basement. In this house, I was subjected to some of the cruelest treatment a child could endure at the hands of both my father and stepmother on a daily basis.

I will never forget the callous and wicked acts to which I was subjected by my step-mother. The fight over winter coats stands out in memory. I was coming from a tropical climate, so of course did not arrive to the United States with any type of a winter wardrobe. As winter began to approach with temperatures hovering around thirty degrees, we were desperate to get some outerwear to keep us warm. Dot had no intention of providing coats for us, yet we pleaded with her. Days turned into weeks which turned into months that we were forced to go out in the winter weather unprotected from the frigid temperature. I still remember that first winter coat from forty years ago after she finally succumbed. It was blue and came down to my thighs and had a hood with a fake fur collar.

How my classmates made fun of that coat! I did not care what it looked like because I finally was warm and got relief from the cold.

Dot would often cook food and hide it under her bed so that we could not have any. Other times, the food she prepared would be made available to her own daughter while she made sure that my sisters and I received nothing. When I went home from school for lunch, there was never any food for me. Dot would buy milk and mark the spot where the milk was last used with a permanent marker, so no one could use it without her knowing. Marcy, however, taught me a trick that whenever I wanted milk, I would pour half a glass from the jug and then refill it with water to the old mark. I am certain Dot never caught on to this strategy as I am sure I would have suffered severe consequences for it. We nonetheless endured hunger many of those days while living in Paterson.

Although Marcy was the usual recipient of my father's physical abuse through the use of his fists, I was the recipient of most of Dot's ire. She would typically, however, make up with me before my father came home because she was afraid that we would report her behavior to him. I am not sure why she was so concerned about his knowing how she treated us when she demonstrated other inappropriate behavior in front of him. One particular scenario I remember well was when my father would play music and drink, my stepmother would insist on dancing with me real close and would grind on me. I was just a young teenager, totally naive to this behavior and certainly ill-equipped to handle it. Yet, she enjoyed being so physical with me no matter how uncomfortable I felt.

Dot was punishing to us. My eldest sister was forced to become a maid to my half-sister, Louise. At eighteen, Joan would cook, clean the house, iron my father and stepmother's clothes, as well as care for Marcy and me. At night, Louise would make her way to the top of the stairs to her pristine room, while my sisters and I would retreat to the basement that was cold in the winter and hot in the summer. The ancient boiler that heated the house made unsettling, scary noises all night. Living in this house certainly did not reflect any sense of its being a real home: a place which offered love, comfort, and security.

My step-mother inflicted much of the cruelty I experienced. My father, however, certainly played a part in it as well. At any random time, he would choose to impose on me physical, verbal or emotional abuse, or a combination thereof. Although Marcy was the recipient on a regular basis, I endured countless bouts of these abuses as well. My father exemplified the word machismo and did not understand the upbringing I had in Guyana. I had spent so many of my formative years with a mother and three sisters. As I learned at an early age to have tremendous respect for women, this would become one of the major distinctions between my father and me. On my fifteenth birthday, my father thought he would introduce me to his world of machismo. He took me to a sleazy strip club, not too far from our house. To this day, decades later, I remember that experience as if it happened yesterday. My father handed the stripper ten dollars and said something to her quietly. She came across the bar towards me wearing a mini skirt, she straddled her legs across my shoulders, and just squatted right in front of me. The woman had nothing on under her mini skirt. I was in pure shock. I jumped off the bar stool and ran the seven blocks home. My father arrived shortly thereafter and gave me one of his all-too-typical beatings for embarrassing him among his friends.

My father exerted his power over Dot as he often did over me. There seemed to be a daily fight between the two of them for one reason or another. Often, it was about me and my sisters. Most times the argument would end in a physical confrontation between my father and stepmother. Dot would always come out on the losing side of those battles as she was often physically and emotionally battered. I recall many days where he would have her running around the block in just a thin nightgown trying to get away from him. Had he caught her on those occasions, my father would have inflicted a terrible beating on her. Our being brought to the United States was undoubtedly an arrangement between Dot and my father which was based on an understanding that once we were brought to the United States, the same courtesy would be extended to her family. Although it was Dot's citizenship that would allow for our immigration, it was my father's control of the household that dictated how this was going to happen. Once the arrangement had been fulfilled, the next step in the process was to get rid of my sisters and me. My sister Joan was to be shipped off to the United States Air Force. Without Joan, who was a comforting and stabilizing presence for me in the home, things would start to spiral out of control. Dot would become meaner to me and Marcy. Within a matter of weeks of Joan's departure, Marcy, who was not quite yet seventeen, would forcefully be shipped off to join the Air Force as well. Joan and Marcy, who were my only bastions of comfort, support, and defense, were gone. I was to be the only one left at home to bear the brunt of my father and stepmother's endless confrontations against each other which were then taken out on me.

Joan, Marcy and I lived on the front line and became a casualty of my father and Dot's battles. We all carry the scars of that dreadful one-and-a-half years of our lives. I know the bitterness they each carry in their hearts for my father, and so I believe the actions of my father have permanently scarred my sisters and destroyed the bonds of our family. I know for a fact those actions have caused irreparable damage to me. In his warped mind, my father continues to believe we are solely responsible for the events that have inflicted this damage, and so he claims no responsibility. To what degree that damage extends, I cannot quantify, but the result of those experiences has certainly made me a dysfunctional adult. The unbearable conditions I endured which ultimately galvanized me to escape my father's house created a chain of events which magnified the pain I suffered. To those who know my father, they would all agree, that even to this day, he lives in an alternate reality. Although he cannot, or chooses not to see the truth, this cannot excuse him from the irreversible damage he has caused. I was a male child and knew how many times terrible things happened to me because a positive male figure was missing from my life. Without a positive role model influence, children grow up like a boat without a rudder. As I endured life in my father's house, I had no one to guide, encourage or protect me.

CHAPTER 7

LIFE IS NO BED OF ROSES

"I have spent my life judging the distance between
American reality and the American dream."

- Bruce Springsteen

I graduated Public School 25 in Paterson, New Jersey in the spring of 1979 and had a choice of applying to Eastside High, Wayne Technical or Paterson Catholic. I was not technically inclined, so Wayne Tech was a not an option. The infamous Joe Clark, featured in the movie *Lean On Me* was the principal at Eastside High, and he was on a mission to turn that school around as it was one of the worst in the nation at that time. There were gangs, weapons, drugs and a host of other problems at that school. Eastside was pretty much in the news every day, and not for anything positive. Being able to fight back or at least being willing to fight back was a requirement to attend that school. The principal would chain the doors shut in the morning and guards with metal detectors were stationed all around the school while Mr. Clark would walk around with a bullhorn and bark orders at students and teachers alike. Knowing my personality and acknowledging my small physique and stature, I knew I would never make it in that vicious environment. So, by the process of elimination, Paterson Catholic High School was my only option. I believe at this point God actively stepped into my life for in a few months I would meet Father Tom, the greatest influence in my life.

I applied for high school in the summer of 1979, one year after I had left Guyana. I told my father I wanted to attend Paterson Catholic High School, but he made it crystal clear that he did not have the money to send me to private school. This response was made notwithstanding the fact that my younger half-sister was attending the most prestigious Catholic school in the city. Nevertheless, with determination on my side, I applied to Paterson Catholic and was accepted. I decided to get a job to pay my tuition for high school. Having a job has always saved me. Employment is not only a source of money, it is also a source of worth, pride, and independence. Even if the job is not the one you want, you take it until you can do better. If you don't see a way to do better, then go back to school to acquire the skills necessary to find the employment you are looking for. For me, it has always been about doing what needs to be done in order to reach the goal. At this particular time, the goal was to be independent and be able to pay my tuition.

As I was barely fifteen years old, my options for employment were limited. I was hired at the neighborhood pharmacy on the recommendation of my eldest uncle who had known the owner for many years. I started working at the local pharmacy on Trenton Avenue in Paterson. My first assignment was to sweep the sidewalks in front of the store. I eagerly stepped into the role of street sweeper. Although I was the first person of color to work there, my work ethic quickly caught the attention of my boss who truly liked me and appreciated my efforts. I was quickly reassigned to stocking the store and ultimately, a few months later, to working the register. I worked six days a week, Monday through Saturday, from 4 p.m. to 8 p.m. My meager paycheck was just enough to cover my tuition at Paterson Catholic as well as my bus pass to school.

One particular day on the job, I experienced a life-changing event. It was about 6:45 p.m. and the pharmacy would normally close at 7 p.m. Three young men came in and separated from each other. One made his way to the front of the store, one stayed at the back and one came to the register at which point I approached him to see how I could assist. In response to his asking for some cough syrup, I turned to get him a bottle. Just as I looked back to hand it to him, he pulled out a gun from under his jacket. It was the first time in my life I had ever seen a gun. He insisted that I lead him to the pharmacist in order for the safe to be opened. Once it was opened, he then proceeded to steal drugs and money. Afterward, he made the pharmacist lay on the floor and had me hand over the cash from the register. When he amassed all that he came for, he made me lay on the floor, took the barrel of the gun and pulled the back of my shirt down to see if I was wearing a necklace that he could also steal. I still remember the coldness of that metal against my neck. By the grace of God, the three men let me, my cousin and the pharmacist be, took the cash and drugs and left the store. After that encounter, I truly began to believe that God must have a greater purpose for my life as he allowed me to live through that experience. I have held onto that conviction with more and more fervor over the years as there have been numerous other life-threatening occasions through which God has allowed me to survive.

On a more consistent basis, I had to contend with the ongoing abuse inflicted by my father. I suppose I reminded my father of many things he did not want to be reminded of, including issues between him and my mother. I possess many of my mother's features and some of her personality as well, so perhaps just looking at me was enough of a reminder. He would beat me at the slightest provocation. Despite my slight build and weighing barely over one hundred pounds, he would hit me like a man. The worst of this abuse occurred days after a party that he hosted for the family at his house. There was plenty of drinking and revelry, and he got drunk and cursed out his ex-wife, my mother, for all the family to hear. This, of course, highly upset me. As angry as I was, I knew not to say a word because I knew that it would result in a terrible beating. Instead, I retreated to the basement and shared my feelings concerning what he had said about my mother with one of my cousins. I told her that when I grew up, I would right the wrongs he had done to me, my sisters and mother. Unfortunately, my cousin shared those details with her mother, my father's sister, who in time would share this information with my father.

One day shortly thereafter, as I sat in class at Paterson Catholic, there was announcement over the high school's public address system. The announcer said, "Robert Lawrie please report to the front office."

When I arrived, I saw my father standing there almost blue with rage. I knew I was in a world of trouble. The beating, which I still remember to this day, started in my father's car. Once we began to back out of the parking space, without his saying a word to me, he tore out of the school parking lot and headed to Route 20 toward our house. I knew a beating was about to come, so I began to mentally and physically prepare myself. At the point when we were on the highway and out of sight of the school, my father immediately started questioning me. When an answer that I gave did not suit him or was contrary to what he heard, he would ball his fist and hit me. I took multiple punches on the way home, along with a brutal cursing about my mother. I sat there and shut my mouth in preparation for what I knew was coming once we got to the house. My father tore into the driveway, parked the car and marched me up the front steps into our house. I still remember the trepidation of trying to climb those stairs that day, anticipating the beating that I knew was coming. Once in the house, he grabbed all one hundred pounds of me by the back of my shirt and threw me into a coat rack by the door. Upon impact, my chin connected with a metal rod which promptly opened a gash in my chin. As I lay on the ground bleeding, he hit me some more. He cursed and ranted about what a whore my mother was and what a loser I would be in life. I knew he would beat me into a pulp if I fought back, so I continued to endure, covering and taking the punches. This is the same man I adored as a little boy. I remember when he would take me on the back of his motorcycle to the farm he had a few miles from our house. On one such ride to the farm, he drove his bike into the back of a truck and he fell off onto the ground. Miraculously, the bike stayed upright and I somehow managed to fall off the bike without being hurt. I ran to him as he lay unconscious and began pouring water on him, begging him not to die. Now, here he was all these years later, beating the life out of me with a demonic rage. I truly hated that man that day. He actually had the audacity in a later conversation to say that he knew he was hard on me, but that he did those things to make me successful. I can think of a plethora of ways that parents can inspire and motivate their children to be successful outside of physical and mental abuse.

Despite the fact that this was a time when my life was literally being beaten out of me, it is when I began to establish a relationship with God. This relationship would last and flourish for the remainder of my life. It has ultimately saved me. As the abuse intensified in my father's home, I took up running. I ran every afternoon when I came home from school and as I ran, I would pray. Running mitigated some of the mental, psychological and emotional pain that became a staple in my life back then and has continued throughout my life to this day. While running, there is a cleansing of both body and spirit. Running has helped me escape from life's miseries. While I run, I pray to God. I ask for strength and for Him to guide me so that I can walk in His ways. I suppose there is a metaphor in the idea of running away from evil and towards goodness. Although I pray at other times as well, I feel the most connected to God when I run. It was on this day, after this beating from my father, when I truly began my journey in running to be one with God.

Amid the physical and emotional abuse that I endured at the hand of my father and stepmother, I was also forced to receive an unintended education about sex. My father and stepmother had sponsored and brought to the United States my stepmother's niece and two nephews as part of the agreement they had to help the family immigrate to the United States. Brenda, my stepmother's niece, was about sixteen at the time. My father showed her all kinds of attention, beginning even several years earlier when she was only a thirteen-year-old teenager living in Guyana. I would later find out that this man, who by definition I must call my father, was having a sexual relationship with this underage girl.

I never had a girlfriend. My life was a constant struggle for survival and trying to get through high school while holding down a job. I had no interest in sex, nor would I have known what to do if given the chance. Yes, my friend Danny and I would look at a few adult magazines, but never the idea of engaging in sex. Brenda and her brothers, Troy and Krish, my stepmother's family, were like relatives to us. We lived together and shared the tumultuous life with my father and stepmother. Brenda, I suppose, saw me differently. I was a virgin and extremely shy. I remember my father thinking I was gay as I had never expressed any interest in girls. He even went as far as arranging for a neighborhood girl, Leila, to lure me into the basement to engage in a sexual encounter. It was not, however, a successful effort as I fought like hell and managed to get out of that basement. I actually hit that girl with a stickball bat Danny and I used to play with over the long summers off the wall of P.S. 25 in order to keep her off me.

My first true sexual encounter occurred in my father's house when I was fifteen. One night while we were all watching TV in the basement, Brenda came and laid next to me. I did not give it a second thought because I had no clue that she was interested in me and again saw her as a relative. I even wonder if my father put her up to it as he had with Leila in order to prevent his great fear that I would become gay. I fell asleep and during the course of the night, I felt a hand caressing my body under the sheets. While her brothers slept in the bunk next to ours, Brenda woke me up and started to caress my body and took my hands and put them on her breasts. As she continued to caress me and take our clothes off, she turned on her side and guided me into her. I immediately was in love, or at least thought I was. This was my first sexual encounter and whatever doubts my father or anyone else had about my sexuality were put to rest. Notwithstanding all the ugly names he has called me over the years, that experience with Brenda firmly set my own identity; I was not gay. Not that it would have made one bit of difference to me, but it would have killed my homophobic father had his namesake, and only son, been gay.

After that encounter, Brenda and I became inseparable. I would walk to the bus stop daily to meet her, the bus stop being some three miles from the house. I would do everything to be around her as she was my oasis of happiness in a desert of abuse, strife and stress. I cannot thank her enough for those few months of happiness in an otherwise horrendous, nightmarish year and a half of my life.

I undoubtedly made Brenda a huge part of my world from that singular encounter: a pattern that I have maintained and will continue for the rest of my life. Every time I sleep with someone I feel as though I am in love with them, to the point where it almost destroys me. My life and my being become subservient to or absorbed by my lover's life. I consequently lose myself when I believe I am in love. All of my efforts and concern focus exclusively on my partner. I have never known how to love with conditions. I never learned to limit the love in my heart. Whatever and whomever I have loved, it is and continues to be boundless. If I could change my perspective on love, I would not—despite how much that level of loving has cost me. It has without a doubt cost me everything a person can think of, but I still believe in giving nothing less than my whole being to the one who loves me. I therefore know that I can never love another person in a romantic way again. My later experiences would make that a necessary condition for my very survival.

Not only did my happiness with Brenda not last, but my idealistic view of love was sullied at an early age. I woke up one morning and made my way to the upstairs bathroom. My father's bedroom door was open, but I did not look in because I was intently focused on getting in to use the restroom. My father, however, was in the restroom standing over the bathroom sink washing his penis. I retreated as he closed the door in my face. As I made my way back to the basement, I looked into my father's room and there was Brenda half naked and smiling at me sheepishly from under the sheets. I then learned that Brenda and my father had been having an affair, even before she had moved to the United States. Later, long after I had moved out, my father ended up having a child with Brenda, his wife's niece, which he blamed on me, notwith-standing the fact that she was born years after I had left the house. This event was my first encounter with heartbreak as I was crushed by the actions of Brenda and my father. My innocence was destroyed at a very early age never to be regained. Sadly, the excruciating hurt which I felt that morning has been repeated over and over in a perpetual cycle throughout my life—even to the present. With time, the hurt has become more and more intense to the point where I became suicidal as a result of the hurt inflicted by the last person I would ever love.

CHAPTER 8

A TRUE FATHER EMERGES

"Our sorrows and wounds are healed only when we touch
them with compassion."

- Buddha

The days at my father's house continued with the same routine that included no love or affection along with consistent mental and physical abuse. My world became one of just surviving. The event that changed this course, as well as my life forever, occurred during the second year I lived in Paterson. One night near midnight, my father came in from work as he would normally do and stormed into the basement. He proceeded to curse at me and carry on because I forgot to take out the garbage. This was not out of the ordinary for him. In fact, it had become quite customary for me not to sleep until I knew he was in from work. I never knew what attitude he would be coming home with and that the slightest provocation would set him off. I could never sleep with that uncertainty. So, I would only sleep once I saw the light go off in the kitchen upstairs and I heard him head up to his room. My father was a total and uncontrollable tyrant in every aspect of the word. As he continued to shout and threaten me in the middle of the night, I realized I had reached my tipping point and that I had had enough. Consequently, I got out of bed and picked up my school backpack into which I put my school shoes, my two school uniforms and two changes of clothing. I then made my way out of the basement and my father's life. I did not say a word to him as I made my way up the basement stairs. I would not see him again for the next seven years, and he did not care. Quite honestly, after what I endured at his hands, neither did I. My father's parting words to me as I left were, "I will see you in the gutter." Naturally, he had to hurl one last insult at me. Funny thing, those words have continued to motivate me all these years. Since that night I always strive to be the best that I can be.

I walked down my street and turned left onto the main road. It was the middle of the night, and I recall saying to myself, "Okay Mr. Big Man, what will you do now? Where will you go?" My life would never be the same after I walked out of my father's house. Looking back, I now realize that this was a pivotal moment in my life when my entire personality, attitude and behavior transformed. I was not even sixteen years old and was all alone on the street with nowhere to go.

The only person within walking distance that I thought might help me was my Aunt Mary. She accepted me for a few days, but her one-bedroom apartment could not handle both her family and me. Additionally, my father pressured her to put me out. I was fortunate, however, as her landlord agreed to rent me a room in his house, the same house where my aunt lived. At this time, I was a sophomore in high school. I did not know how to cook or wash and now had to live on my own. My meals consisted of cereal, peanut butter and banana sandwiches, coffee, and soup from a can. These bare necessities were supplemented by whatever I could afford to purchase with the few measly dollars I had left over after I paid tuition and the three hundred dollars in rent which the landlord charged me. I had a little black and white television in my room, a little radio my cousin had given me, and my bicycle the landlord allowed me to keep downstairs. I hung on tenaciously, but I knew something had to give. I could not afford my tuition, bus pass, food and rent all on the paltry paycheck I received every two weeks. I started to fall behind on my tuition payments.

One day while in class, toward the end of the day, over the dreaded public address system, I heard the announcer say, "Robert Lawrie please report to the bursar's office." I knew this was not going to be good because I knew I was almost three months behind on my tuition payments. I made my way down to the office and met with Mrs. Birney, the bursar. She informed me as kindly as she could that I was two months behind in my tuition and fast approaching a third. She continued that as much as everyone liked having me at Paterson Catholic, I would have another week to come current on my tuition or I would not be able to remain enrolled. I had a decision to make: eat or pay tuition. As much as staying in school was important to me, I chose the former believing I really did not even a choice. This of course meant that I would be kicked out of Paterson Catholic which would result in an abrupt end to my dream of using a degree from a school of distinction as a springboard for getting into one of the better colleges. Rutgers University was my dream school and I was determined to get in, one way or another. But now I was faced with a huge hurdle if I could not remain at Paterson Catholic. I do not know what drove me to appreciate education as much as I did then because only two years prior I was living in Guyana and absolutely hated everything about school. Yet here I was, in just two short years, dreaming of getting into college. I knew good grades at Paterson Catholic would be the key to getting into college and so I endeavored to succeed in high school. My years since this circumstance have only validated my understanding of the value of education. My academic pursuits in reaching the highest of educational goals have not only helped me weather some of the most turbulent storms, but they have also enabled me to advance up the socio-economic ladder.

When I officially received the expected news from Mrs. Birney, it was the end of the day and no students were around. I went to my locker, sat on the floor and started to cry uncontrollably. I was fed up and tired. This occasion was one of the few times in my life when I felt sorry for myself. I rarely ever sink to this emotion as it serves no purpose other than to sap your motivation to change your situation. But on that day, I truly saw no way out. I try to remind myself that the longer a person dwells in self-pity, the longer it takes to recover and move on with life. Sad things will always happen. That is just life's reality. It is how one deals with that reality that is important. The ability to pick oneself up and move forward in spite of sad events is an exercise in true courage. When one is beaten down enough times, it is very easy to stay down. It is easy to get to the point where you become so tired of trying that it is an effort to just exist. It is at that point that it is most important to find a way to move forward. The best way to do that is to find or create a purpose in your life. It needs to be something worthwhile to get you up out of bed every day. There have been many days in my life when I just wanted all the troubles to end or when I wished for my childhood days when my mother would make everything better. As an adult, that is never a realistic option, so we must find a way to pick ourselves up and take care of the situation on our own. On this day, however, I was not sure I would be able to do that.

As I processed the information that Mrs. Birney relayed to me and thought about my options, I sat on the floor of the hallway. The bell had rung, and the school was vacant. I was all alone in that empty hallway, and as empty as the building was, I was equally as empty inside. When I was a child growing up in Guyana, I never envisioned the life I was now living. It is sad how when I resided in Guyana, life in the United States was portrayed "as a bed of roses." My mother was fond of that saying, but I then learned that nothing was further from the truth for me or for many others like myself who came to this great country seeking the American dream. I did not have the energy to get up, to open my locker or to leave. I missed the school bus and was going to have to walk to the pharmacy some six miles away. This meant that I would be late for the little job that sustained me; the job that I could not afford to lose.

As I sat there crying I heard someone calling my name. I picked up my head and saw that it was Father Tom, the assistant principal. He asked me why I was crying. I refused to say at first as I was terribly embarrassed, but I eventually acceded and explained the situation with which I was confronted. After a bit more prodding, I went on to divulge most of my story since my arrival from Guyana except for the beatings I received from my father. Perhaps I should have told him that too, but as it was only five months since I had left my father's house, it was still too fresh and too personal. Nonetheless, despite this being one of the lowest days of my life, my conversation with Father Tom began a relationship that would prove to be the greatest influence on me. It would become a relationship that would last for decades and stretch over continents. More importantly, it would become a relationship that not only taught me the skills I would need to survive and thrive in America, but it also taught me what it meant to live and love as a man with compassion and kindness for all of humanity. He taught me how to expect the most out of myself and to be grateful for all of my blessings. Father Tom truly shaped me into the man I have become and his legacy lives on as I teach those values to my students while I echo his words and deeds.

Father Tom left in what seemed to be a state of disbelief, and I did not see him again for a while. About one week later, I was again called to the bursar's office. With tears in my eyes, I made my way once more to see Mrs. Birney. As I walked into her office, she asked me why I was crying. I told her that it was obvious as to the reason she called me down to see her: to ask me to leave Paterson Catholic as I still had not paid my tuition. To my surprise and disbelief, Mrs. Birney told me to stop crying, and again to my surprise, told me that my tuition had been paid. The only reason she called me to her office was to give me the receipt for my paid tuition. I was dumbfounded! As I knew I had not paid my tuition, I asked her to tell me who had paid it. She said that the person wanted to stay anonymous, but after pleading with her and telling her I only wanted to express my gratitude, she gave in and told me it was Father Tom. It was at that moment that my faith in God was sealed forever and would never be shaken. And, for the first time in my life, I realized that I genuinely loved another human being. The love I felt for him was not the cursory puppy love I felt for Brenda, nor was it the love I was supposed to feel for my family notwithstanding the dysfunction and abuse. No, the love I had, and still hold, for Father Tom transcends familial bonds and physical connections. It was a love rooted in care and concern as well as mutual trust and respect. So began a relationship with the greatest person I have ever known, and one who would, without question, have the greatest impact on me.

After I dried my tears and spoke with Mrs. Birney, I immediately went over to Father Tom's office to thank him for the kindness he had extended on my behalf. He accepted my thanks and said he understood my plight and how I could have fallen behind in my tuition payments. He asked if he could give me a ride home. Since I had now missed my school bus and was late for my job, I gladly accepted. When Father Tom came to my address and saw where I was living, he was in a state of shock. My neighborhood, one of the worst in Paterson, was lined with dirty and dilapidated row houses that were crowded with multiple immigrant families. The disbelief intensified after seeing my room in which my only worldly possessions included a 12-inch black and white television, a fan, because there was no air conditioning, and a few articles of clothing. Father Tom was then convinced of my story. He left shortly thereafter and asked me to come to his office the following day.

I did as Father Tom requested and went to his office, an activity I would continue to do on many other days while I attended Paterson Catholic. Father Tom sat me down and told me he had a home for me if I was willing to move. Because I was behind on my rent, that was the best news I had been given since Mrs. Birney informed me about my tuition. So, I gladly accepted the offer. I worked that evening at the pharmacy after which Father Tom came by to get me. He collected my television and the few pieces of clothes I had, while I grabbed my bike from downstairs. He put the bike in the back of his car and we proceeded to the rectory at Newman Prep in Wayne, New Jersey, where he was the parish priest.

Wayne was one of the more exclusive cities in New Jersey— truly the other side of the tracks. When we arrived, Father Tom gave me my own room surrounded by books, which I eagerly began to read. In the morning Father Tom gave me a bowl of raisin bran cereal and drove me to school. This now became my new home.

CHAPTER 9

LIVING AMONG THE MEN OF GOD

"We must accept finite disappointment,
but never lose infinite hope."

- Martin Luther King, Jr.

Providing me a place to live with my own room was the first blessing of a countless list of blessings that Father Tom bestowed on me throughout my life. He arranged for me to enroll in the work study program at Paterson Catholic, so I was able to get a job in the school cafeteria. I would report an hour before school began to set up the tables for breakfast and then dismantle them afterwards. Although this might seem like an insignificant responsibility, it helped me tremendously. The income helped pay my school tuition and, almost as importantly, it offered me the opportunity to obtain a hot morning meal.

My days at the Newman Prep rectory were lonely as I was surrounded only by priests. Most days, Father Tom was out and about doing a hundred different things. I did, however, read a lot. Above all, I was safe. I remember when the weather was warm, I would sit on the grass behind the rectory and read. I read everything I could get my hands on at that time. I still do. Reading was my window to the world. Understanding that my experiences were limited, I knew that by reading I could not only learn new things, but I could vicariously experience the world. This love for reading activated a thirst for knowledge that I have never seemed to be able to quench.

While at Newman Prep, I met a younger priest, Father Tomas. He was Portuguese and was the student advisor at Fairleigh Dickinson University. He was very young at heart and fun to be around. I tried my first alcoholic drink with Father Tomas. He took me to New York City and we ended up at an historic Irish pub called McSorley's. I was introduced to beer for the first time and had the time of my life on what was really my first social night out, never mind that I was underage. Even though I had never been to a pub before, what stands out in my memory is the restroom. As women were not allowed entrance to this establishment until 1970, there was only one restroom and it was not gender specific. The men would use the urinals and the women the stalls. It appeared that the regulars who frequented McSorley's did not seem fazed by this arrangement. For those of us who were not used to such a set-up, however, it did take some getting used to when ladies would walk past men using the urinals. Although I do believe this arrangement has since changed to one that is more typical, at the time it was quite unique. If Father Tom ever knew of that excursion, he never let on. Although it transpired decades ago, I remember that night as though it happened yesterday and will always smile when I think of Father Tomas and that outing.

Father Tom spoke to me often, usually in the evenings when he came home and after he had his two daily drinks of scotch and water. Once during one of those daily evening chats, he said he would not be able to keep me at the rectory any longer because he did not think it was the ideal place to raise a teenage boy. He told me that he knew a fellow priest at a parish called Saint John's in Paterson where there was a place I could stay and be safe. I trusted Father Tom as he had been good to me since the first day I met him and, as I had not heard a single word from my father in all the time since I left his home,

I agreed to the offer. I moved to a building on the grounds of Cathedral of St. John the Baptist in Paterson, New Jersey pastored by the now infamous Monsignor Jose Alonso. The building was a temporary shelter that housed homeless Central American illegal and undocumented aliens. Father Jose was a revered and well-respected priest when I went to Saint John's, but he was harboring a terrible secret: one in which I became an unwitting partner and victim. A secret that I harbored for almost four decades of my life. A secret that would devastate my life, ruin my relationships with those nearest and dearest to me and almost push me over the edge. Ironically, it has been my trust in God that has sustained me.

Monsignor Alonso, or Father Jose, as he was referred to by most of the teenage boys of the parish, was grotesquely overweight and was terribly mean at times. I had occasionally seen his temper on display over the most trivial of things. He spoke in a quiet, controlled and authoritarian voice, and he had a commanding spirit about him. On Father Tom's request, Father Jose gave me a room on the second floor of the building overlooking the side of the church. It was just that: a room. The walls were bare except for a crucifix, along with a bed and several blankets. The mattress of the bed warped in the middle and took a little bit of getting accustomed to in order to get a restful night's sleep. It was a good thing that I had gotten used to sleeping in a hammock in my younger days in Guyana. This bed did not prove to be too much of a transition for me. The thick, brown, woolen blankets would become my best friends as winter approached. There was no door that could be locked, but that did not concern me as I had no real possessions at that time except for my faithful old 12-inch black and white television with the rabbit ears antennae. There was a shower that everyone used and a kitchen downstairs where anyone could cook. I remember there was a wooden table in the kitchen and chairs around it. I would spend many nights at that table studying and writing papers to get through high school.

Although I had a television, after saving a few dollars, I was able to buy a Walkman. In the era predating MP3 players and digitalized playlists, this precursor to today's sources of music served the same purpose at that time. This beautiful machine kept me company during the few hours in which I was not working or studying in order to get through Paterson Catholic. My preferred genre then, as it remains today, was country and western music. I spent many nights listening to singers like Charlie Pride, Hank Williams and Jim Reeves until I fell asleep.

I had to hustle my meals as best I could. I was fortunate to be able to count on a free hot breakfast every morning at school because of my cafeteria job. Father Tom typically brought me some kind of meal for lunch which we ate together. Dinner, on the other hand, was the most challenging of meals. On occasion, Beatriz, a kind lady who worked at the convent, as I referred to the building where I lived, would cook and save me food which I could later have for dinner.

She called me Roberto and always treated me well. More often than not, however, I would find dinner on my own. This was quite the challenge as I lacked the skills to cook and the money to buy a meal. I guess that helps to explain why I was rail thin back then. After my tuition and bus pass were paid, whatever spare change that remained would often go to purchasing a Danish pastry with a cup of coffee at the pharmacy where I continued to work. Often, I would have to wolf down that "meal" while I was changing my clothes in the basement from school uniform to work uniform. Up to that point, my boss never knew about my situation and other responsibilities, but I remember his startling me one day as I was getting changed and devouring my food. That tough Italian pharmacy owner, for the first time since I had been working there, showed me compassion. All he did when he saw me eating and changing was tear up and walk back up the stairs from the basement. I had thought for sure he was going to yell at me for wasting time when I was already on the clock, but God knows I was doing the best I could. I believe he recognized that.

The church and rectory where I lived were located on the corner of Grand and Main Streets in the middle of downtown Paterson. The cathedral itself was perhaps one of the largest buildings in that area. It was cavernous and ornate, constructed in the typical Gothic style. The cathedral was erected in the second half of the nineteenth century to serve the burgeoning Irish Catholic immigrant population that was beginning to dominate the city at the time. It was built in an area that was known as the "Dublin" section of Paterson. By the time I moved to Saint John's, the building itself was well over one hundred years old. Now instead of serving a large Irish population, it was serving a large Hispanic population as the Irish majority had long left Paterson by this time. It struck me as a cold haven for the unwanted and unwelcome entities in America. At this point, I did not feel very welcome in America, so in retrospect, perhaps it was where I belonged.

The building attached to the rectory that would be my residence for the next few months was home to an eclectic collection of other homeless people like myself. Many of them were immigrants and most of them were illegal from South and Central America. I was perhaps the only person in that building that was living in America legitimately. I watched those poor people struggle as much as I did to keep their heads above water. I believe living among those other immigrants at that time gave me a deep empathy for the poor and underscores my continued drive to make a difference with that segment of the population. Poverty has always been and continues to be a tremendous burden to bear on too many people in our country. For most of them, they are never able to escape out from under that weight to reach any level of financial security.

Few people living at Saint John's spoke English fluently. They pretty much kept to themselves and no one made friends.

Everyone was always on guard and high alert because no one really knew one person from the next. It was never clear whether one would be a potential friend or foe. So, it was safer not to make personal connections. I learned that the hard way when I befriended an older resident at Saint John's. He taught me how to fry eggs. Considering that I had zero cooking skills, I wound up eating eggs almost every night for dinner. I appreciated the cooking competency and what I thought was friendship, but that "friend" ultimately ended up stealing the only luxury I afforded myself in those days: my Walkman.

On occasion, Father Jose took all of us out to his favorite diner, located on Route 46 in Clifton. Going on these outings to that diner was the greatest treat I could imagine. Father Jose would sit up front and would have one of his "favored" young men drive while the rest of us would cram into the back of his car. He would treat us to whatever we wanted for dinner and Father Jose would always get a Napoleon pastry for dessert. There would be a price to pay later for this treat. Some of the young men that went on these dinner outings had special privileges and would go back to Father Jose's private quarters to "watch television." As I look back, I remember Father Jose as always being surrounded by a group of young teenage boys like myself. Whether it be at the diner or having his fat, swollen feet massaged, Father Jose always liked having young teenage boys around him. I remember one special boy of whom he was quite fond and referred to as "El Gato." He lived in the rectory with Father Jose in a room upstairs and was always chosen to be his driver. I now can surmise that El Gato paid dearly for that "favored" status due to his constant proximity to Father Jose as well as those special privileges bestowed on him. I was not part of that crew, and if I only knew what was taking place behind closed doors at that time, I would never have even wanted to be part of that crew. Regardless, I, too, was soon to be "favored" by Father Jose.

As winter approached, I noticed that the heat was not being utilized. As September, October, and then November came, there was still no heat. By November the old, dreary building was freezing. I would cover myself at night with three or four blankets to stay warm as the temperature dropped inside the building. The temperature inside always seemed to equal the temperature outside. I would shower in the frigid water to the point of being clean in as little time as I could so as not to freeze to death. A quick splash with the water, a quick lather of soap, followed by a quick rinse and I was out of that shower. Those were some very difficult days. I did not complain to Father Tom because it was still better than going back to my father's house and being subjected to the physical and verbal abuse that was part of my daily existence there.

However, in late November of that same year I became ill. I had a stomach virus and a terrible fever. To make matters worse, since my Walkman had been stolen, the only company I had now was the television in my room: the old 12-inch black and white with the rabbit ears antennae that barely worked. I truly was miserable. Ultimately, I became so sick that I started missing school and work. I realized that I needed help and medication. So, I went to Father Jose. He suggested that I walk across the street to the pharmacy and pick up some suppositories for my stomach ache and fever. What did I know about which medication was necessary for a stomach ache and fever? After all, I rarely got sick and when I did, someone else always took care of me. Obediently, I went and got the suppositories as Father Jose had instructed me to do. He brought me into the rectory to his private quarters, which were immaculate and draped in what appeared to me to be royal trappings. This was quite contradictory to the image of the humble priest that he portrayed to the public. His room had a huge king-size bed covered with a white bedspread laced with tiny pink flowers, contrasted by dark brown and purple drapes to keep the sun out, a large color television and carpeted floors. Most strikingly, he had heat in his room. The temperature felt to be a comfortable 72 degrees. Nothing about Father Jose's quarters resembled anything close to my own room. It was the opposite of where I lived, but I was quite happy to be afforded this luxury, even if it were to be for a short time.

Upon entering his room, Father Jose made me lie horizontally across the bed. I was sixteen, rail thin and sick as a dog. I complied. As a Catholic monsignor this man was a pillar in the predominantly Hispanic neighborhood that Paterson had become. I trusted him implicitly. Why shouldn't I have? He took the suppository from the foil wrapper and told me to take off all of my clothes. As he spread my butt apart, I felt him probing with his fingers and slipping the suppository inside, all the while asking me how it felt. I trusted this man because he was a priest and a colleague of Father Tom's. Before I fully realized what had happened, he had pinned me against the bed with all of his grossly overweight 250 pounds on top of me. I never felt such pain as he forced his penis into my butt. I felt the weight of that disgusting man against my body. I know he ripped my anus because I was in pain for many days afterward and saw blood in my underwear. Even going to the bathroom over the next several days was unbearable. As I think back, I never could figure out why I did not scream or fight back at that moment. I suppose my need to have a roof over my head and a bed to sleep in weighed more than what was happening to me. I did not want to be on the streets anymore and I certainly did not want to go back to my father's house. I just allowed my mind to separate itself from the physical act that was being forced upon my body.

I was raped. I still can't believe it happened to me, the young boy that had trusted and revered priests my entire life. I was so proud to know that I was a student at a Catholic school. Yet, here it was that I had now been raped by someone

I so admired. In contrast, Father Tom gave me back my life and represented all that was good, while here was Father Jose, a supposed savior, who used the trust I had afforded him to take away the security I had begun to create. He represented such evil as he committed this heinous act against me.

When he finished with his business, Father Jose did not say much to me. I simply put my underwear and pants back on and went back to my room. I hated everyone and everything at that time. I hated life itself. I cried for hours on end after this episode. I felt more alone than I have ever felt in my entire life. I questioned whether I was at fault for what happened to me. I questioned why I left Guyana. I questioned my sexuality. I questioned my purpose for being in this life, and most importantly, I questioned why God would put me through such an experience. Although I never questioned my faith in God, I did question His purpose for me. The next day at school I asked Father Tom if I could leave Saint John's with the excuse that the severe cold was making me sick. All I wanted was to get away, so I would never have to go through that experience again or be reminded of it. I was disheartened when my plea was not immediately realized. I never said a word to anyone at that time about what had transpired with Father Jose, who years later was convicted on multiple counts of child molestation and sent to prison where he lived out the remainder of his life. There are hundreds of thousands of victims, including myself, who carry the weight of this pain, humiliation and disgrace daily.

The enduring consequences that these experiences have had on my personal well-being as well as my interpersonal relationships continue to negatively impact. However, the human will to survive is bolstered by the mind's ability to suppress painful experiences into the subconscious in order to protect our conscious existence. My past strategy had been to effectively bury painful experiences so that I might continue to function. I would take painful episodes and lock them away in the titanium confines of my mind. Every so often those episodes would manage to escape and cause me unbearable pain. Pain that was so intense, on occasion it would cause me to cry uncontrollably or even to become suicidal, until I could recapture them and lock them away again. I reasoned away the experience with Father Jose for decades in a bid to lead as normal a life as possible. However, in writing this book, I have been compelled to come face to face with those buried memories, and have concluded that I, and I assume other victims as well, never fully heal. However, victims of sexual abuse can learn to confront the nightmares and the shame even if we cannot escape the memories. This may be a difficult task for victims of priests with the added reminders from new stories that continue to come to light and are broadcast in the media. This scandalous behavior has been perpetuated for way too many decades and is most likely far from over. After Pope Francis recently required all thirty-one bishops from Chile to resign, the deplorable behavior exhibited by an alarming number of priests, along with a systemic intent to cover up culpability indicates that there is a long way to go before the Catholic Church puts this nightmare to rest. Although the Church has its burden to carry, the victims carry far heavier burdens, for far longer distances. The physical violation may only have taken a few minutes, but the resulting effect leaves a lifetime of hurt, oftentimes more painful than the physical act itself. At this point, I have learned that sharing my experiences is the best way for me to heal. It forces me to allow those memories to come sweeping forward and ultimately bringing the sense of calm I need. My faith in God has invigorated me to get past this storm and try to help others get past theirs as well. I know that if one truly has faith in an almighty power, then that faith must remain stalwart regardless of what one experiences in life—good or bad. Faith represents the acceptance of a higher power and authority; therefore, we must acquiesce to whatever He gives us. It is the combination of an unshakable faith in a loving God and the use of the memories and scars which I have accumulated that motivates me to push myself beyond whatever artificial boundaries I may have imposed on myself or society has set for me. I have come to realize that the pursuit of education coupled with the potential to positively impact the lives of others will enable me to bypass any limitations I have previously felt and allow me to reach my potential. I have come to believe that through the experience with Father Jose, I was being shaped by fire into what I was meant to be.

I will no longer be a victim living in shame and I hope to encourage others to move past this as well. I believe it is only through communication, awareness, and the accountability of those who commit, excuse, or cover up this reprehensible behavior that the burden of shame can be eased. Those who carry their deep secret, whether it be victims or those in the hierarchy of the Catholic Church, must be encouraged to unveil and address the experience in order to heal the souls of those past victims and prevent the perpetuation of potential future ones. There are countless reticent victims that struggle every day to come to terms with those tragic experiences and whatever negative impact it may have created on their lives as I know it has on mine. It is my hope that there truly is strength in numbers so that through open dialogue, not only can the victims of abuse find some peace, but also so the Catholic Church can restore its name, its mission, and its respect for all clergy.

CHAPTER 10

FOR THE LOVE OF FAMILY

"The bond that links your true family is not one of blood,
but of respect and joy in each other's life."

- Richard Bach

I would spend most of my limited free time while attending Paterson Catholic in Father Tom's office. For me, those times were sanctuary as they provided me not only a place of refuge from the loneliness of growing up without a family, but also with the time to receive the guidance I so desperately needed. One day while in his office, Father Tom told me that he had been searching for a family that he hoped would be an ideal fit for me in terms of teaching me the things I needed to know in order to develop into a well-adjusted teenager. He thought he had found a perfect family from a parish in Paterson where he would occasionally do a service, as their home was within walking distance to Paterson Catholic. It was his opinion that I needed to be in this type of atmosphere, so I could see and experience what a real family felt like. He asked me to visit with them and if I felt comfortable, I could stay there for as long as I liked. I visited with Bob and Maureen Smith and their three children in Paterson and they made me feel more than welcome. Therefore, the next day I packed up my few belongings and moved in with them. The Smiths' home became more than just my permanent address for the next seven years. It gave me a stable, secure home as well as a family to call my own.

Maureen and Bob treated me like one of their own. I was given my very own room, access to a television and a warm fireplace that was often lit. Bob would listen to classical music and I would sit along with him to enjoy it together. I loved sitting back in the den at night when everyone else had gone to sleep and the fireplace was still going. I would read books and dream about my future while the firewood crackled, and the flames shot up into the chimney. I missed my life as a boy in Guyana, but I knew there was no going back. My life was in the United States. It was what my mother had sacrificed so much for. Even though my life had taken a disastrous turn, I was still hopeful for the future. I was sad as I had lost all contact with my mother and siblings, but now I had a new home, a new foster family, Father Tom, and my faith to sustain me.

By this time, I was at the end of my sophomore year in high school and just about two years since I had left my father's house. In return for being brought into Bob and Maureen's home, we made an agreement where I would give them $150 per month for room and board. Despite the fact that I arrived as a stranger to them, they treated me like family. I was brought right into their Irish family culture and traditions. I grew up to love Irish food and music which there was plenty of most Sunday evenings at the house. I even learned the words to most of the Irish songs with "Danny Boy" being my favorite. Those were some of my happiest days. I was taken out to restaurants for family meals, I shot hoops with Bob, played with the children, and celebrated Christmas with gifts under the tree. I had my first true home since I left Guyana. Maureen was beyond good to me and was fiercely protective of me. I loved her immensely. Aside from Father Tom, Maureen has been the greatest influence in my life. I continue to love her even all these years later, perhaps more so, as I can put into perspective the enormity of the task she took on in raising a broken teenager. I will always consider Maureen to be an angel sent by God as she helped shape me and prepare me for the next stage of my life. She helped instill in me the values and confidence I would need to help maneuver my life as I grew to become independent. She and her family showed me the love and support that I had been missing.

As the days and weeks went by, I continued to work and make my way through high school. In addition to the love and support I received from the Smith family, my friendship with Father Tom continued to grow as well. It grew from one of deep respect and gratitude to one of love for a father. By this point, I considered Father Tom my true father, and I believe he considered me like a son, which was demonstrated by the guidance, kindness, and love he bestowed upon me. Although my biological father has made claims about his putting me through college and being tremendously supportive, nothing could be further from the truth. I did not see that man for seven years after I left his house that fateful night. Not only was there never any support, there was not even communication. Instead, it was Father Tom who I saw almost daily. I saw him at school and spent all my free periods in his office discussing an array of topics. It was from these conversations and the time I spent with him that I learned so much about the world and what my place in it should be. He helped define my character and refine my soul. Many times, in my adult life when things would become challenging, I would call him and ask why things had to be so hard on me and if, in his role as a priest, he could put a good word in with God on my behalf to lighten the load I was carrying. He had a standard answer which I can still hear him saying: "I'm in sales, not management." Father Tom helped me to accept the world, to adapt to it and to push me to reach my potential. Although it has been God that has given me the strength to rise above the many tribulations I have faced in life, it has been Father Tom's love and guidance that has kept me on the right path to follow.

As Christmas approached in my junior year of high school, my religion teacher, Father Bradley, and I struck up a friendship. I was very much a loner during my first few years in high school because I was not a typical teenager. Because I was taking care of myself, my mindset was completely different from the average high school student. Due to my adult responsibilities, I tended to relate better to adults than to other teenagers. Father Bradley asked me what I was doing for Christmas and if I wanted to join him for the holiday. He lived within walking distance to the Smiths and directly across from Paterson Catholic, so I accepted his invitation. Maureen had no issue with my going, although I believe if she had known about the Father Jose episode, she would have had a very different response. She even suggested that I bring a bottle of wine as a Christmas gift. After entering the apartment from the outside frigid air, I should have suspected something was wrong as the temperature inside the apartment was about 95 degrees. In this heat, Father Bradley was wearing only his underwear as he came to greet me. The sight of him in just his underwear made me extremely uncomfortable and, in retrospect, I should have left. However, as a seventeen-year-old teenager without much worldly knowledge or a secure foundation, I did not understand my options. I asked Father Bradley about the heat in the apartment to which he said that the thermostat was broken and that was why he was only wearing his underwear. I should have known better especially in light of Father Jose's earlier behavior, yet I stayed.

After watching a movie and talking through the evening, it started to snow and Father Bradley suggested that I should not walk home because it was late and it was very cold outside. He told me I could sleep in his room and he would sleep on the couch. I did not trust him and was very uncomfortable;

however, I relented when he insisted. Notwithstanding the decision to stay, my instincts and the very thought of what Father Bradley might be up to put me on high alert. I was not sick this time and I was not going to be taken advantage of a second time. That mistake was not going to be compounded by my inability to act, like I did last time. This time I swore I would fight if necessary. I was no longer the skinny kid that Father Jose had taken advantage of. By this point, I had started lifting weights and was more than capable of taking care of myself if it came down to a physical confrontation.

I went to his room, turned the lights off, and laid on my back with my eyes closed, but I was not asleep. What priest walks around his apartment in his underwear with a student of his present? How could I trust that behavior? About half an hour later, I saw the door opening and Father Bradley made his way into the room stark naked. He brushed against me as he made his way to the other side of the bed. I was out of there like a bat out of hell. I jumped out of the bed, grabbed my coat, and was out the door before he could say anything to me. I ran all three blocks in the blinding snow home to the Smiths'. Just as I prayed to God the night I ran from my father's house, I prayed with a fervor that night I ran from Father Bradley. When I got home, I immediately told Maureen what Father Bradley had done. She had become like a mother to me and I trusted her. I knew she would protect me like her very own. She suggested I call Father Tom, which I did. I explained to him what had happened, and he was livid. Father Tom was absent from school that next day and Father Bradley did not return to school for a week. When Father Tom did return to school, he told me he had driven over to Father Bradley's home and had punched him in his face. I suspect that was why Bradley was absent from school that entire week as he needed some healing time. That was perhaps the only time that Father Tom, a true man of God, ever resorted to violence. Father Bradley did eventually return to Paterson Catholic, but he kept his distance from me for the rest of my high school years.

As I neared the end of my high school career, I told Father Tom that I wanted to become a priest. He neither encouraged nor discouraged me from that decision, rather all he said was for me to go to college for a year. If I still felt like I wanted to join the priesthood after a year in college, he would do his best to get me into the seminary. Meeting the woman who would become my first wife became my focus during my freshman year of college, so the seminary was not meant to be. In retrospect, it would have been a good decision if I had taken that alternate path. It might have saved me from many of the trials and tribulations I have endured throughout my life. This is one of the many regrets I have, but I continue to trust and believe in God's plan for my existence. I have been subject to many experiences in which I should, by all accounts, have died. God, however, protected and sustained me. The only logical conclusion is that there is some purpose I have yet to fulfill. Therefore, I must exist in order to do so. No matter what happens in my life, I continue to believe and have faith in God and pray to fulfill the purpose He has set out for me.

Father Tom wanted me to attend his alma mater, Saint Francis in Brooklyn, but I wanted to go to Rutgers University. For as long as I can remember, I had dreamed about attending Rutgers, and Father Tom was nonetheless full of pride for me when I ultimately received my acceptance there. I had no plan for how I was going to finance my college education, but I was confident that I was going there one way or another. This was my dream and I knew that my faith allowed me to believe that anything was possible. Between my faith in God and belief in the power of education, I concluded that if my dream to be accepted into Rutgers came true, then I had no doubt there would be a way to make it materialize.

On the day of my graduation from high school, three years after I left my father's house, there was not a single biological family member present at the ceremony. The Smith family as well as Father Tom were the ones supporting me, as I suppose it should have been, since they were the ones who truly helped me reach that milestone. Maureen and Bob took me to an Italian restaurant for a celebratory dinner. The entire family came; indeed, this was a very special occasion. At the end of the dinner, I was given a number of gifts to get me started in college. The last gift Maureen and Bob gave me, however, took my breath away and imprinted on my heart the goodness in people. Maureen handed me a little package. It did not seem like anything special when I opened it, until I saw that it was a bank book. When I looked at the balance, I started to cry. The balance was five thousand and four hundred dollars. The dollar amount was exactly what I had paid in rent from my little job I had at the pharmacy for the three years of high school that I lived with the Smiths. They had now given me back that money not only as a graduation gift but as a way to help me finance my first year at Rutgers University. I cried that day like I had never cried before. I had never felt so loved and touched as I did at that moment. I now had almost half of the tuition for my first year of college. Up to this point, although I was accepted to the university and was determined to go, I had no plan as to how I was going to pay for it. Maureen and Bob's gift reinforced my belief that anything was possible.

The entire Smith family came to drop me off at Rutgers University in the fall of 1983. With my Pell Grants and support from the Educational Opportunity Fund, I was just about able to make it financially through my first year. My tuition, meal plan and housing were covered; however; as I was still short for weekend meals and clothing, I needed to find employment. I really did not care what type of job it was; I just needed to find a way to generate enough income to cover what

I still needed. Soon after the beginning of school, I found work as a server at an Italian restaurant in New Brunswick. I was fortunate to get that job as there were no other people of color on staff. When the manager, Tony, initially saw me he did not want to hire me, but they were busy that night, so he took a chance on me. I worked my backside off. I was literally running from one table to the next with trays of food in my hands. At one point, I fell when I slipped on some oil that had spilled on the floor. I got right back up and continued working. At the end of the night Tony was pleased with my work and allowed me to stay. I suppose Tony appreciated not only my effort but my ability as well. I started working there three nights a week. My undergraduate studies were extremely challenging so the combination of working at the restaurant and trying to keep up with my grades at school was taking a terrible toll. My grades began to slide, and I was put on academic probation. I knew I had to establish a better balance between my work and my academic responsibilities. School now became the priority.

The regulars at the restaurant loved me. I was polite and waited on them hand and foot. At Christmas time, they stuffed my hands with 4 one-hundred-dollar bills. I was their "boy," and I did not mind as long as the dollars were coming in to get me through school. My mind was always on the end game, and I became quite adept at working for the long haul.

While at school, Father Tom would come and pick me up on weekends and bring me to wherever he was assigned. On Saturdays we would play fierce games of racquetball, which I typically lost. We would then go out for dinner. At this point I was just about able to keep up with him with the drinks, but I could never keep up with him on the racquetball court. He also gave me access to any clothes he had in his closet that would fit me. As a student, I never had money for luxuries like nice clothes since whatever money I made from waiting tables and from financial aid went directly to pay for my college education. Father Tom was all too happy to let me take what I wanted, so I would pack them up and bring them back to school with me. In addition to the clothing, he would also give me a little cash to get through the hard times back at school. At this point it had been four years since I heard any word from any member of my biological family. Father Tom continued to take care of me and I found myself trying to be just like him on so many levels.

I survived my freshman year and moved back in with the Smiths for the summer of 1984. I knew I had to make as much money as I could for the upcoming school year. I had taken several prerequisite courses to stay academically eligible at Rutgers and that cost exceeded my financial aid. To compound the need for money, I decided to take additional regular credit hours at Passaic County College during the summer so that I could graduate from Rutgers on time. Father Tom's brother, Frank, gave me a job as a cashier at his convenience store. I would go to school during the day at Passaic County College, go home to the Smiths, catch a few hours of sleep and then cover the twelve-hour overnight shift, from seven in the afternoon to seven the next morning. This routine was difficult to sustain as it often did not allow me time to get even a minimal amount of sleep or to eat. Some nights when I worked, forgive me Frank, I would steal some milk and pie from the store, so I had something to eat for dinner.

One night when I was especially tired because I had been in school all day and worked half the night, I knew driving home would be difficult. I got on the highway dog-tired and was hurrying to get home before I fell asleep. The next thing I heard was a huge bang: I had fallen asleep and crashed the Smith's car into the median. I know I should have felt grateful that I was not injured. However, knowing I had caused this damage to Maureen's car made me feel like I would have preferred to be dead. She not only treated me with kindness, but Maureen covered for me with Bob. I had only my guilt with which to contend.

After surviving such a hectic summer, I went back to Rutgers in the fall and was given a scholarship as well as a position as a resident adviser. This position enabled me to pay for my room and board. It also gave me a little stipend. It was an ideal arrangement because it allowed me to make my ends meet plus I had the benefit of the privacy of my own room. Between the few additional dollars earned and the girlfriend I now had, this school year afforded me a little bit of added pleasure. On a rare occasion, I would take the train from New Brunswick into New York City, most often frequenting the Village. Whether it was to eat out, see a live music performance or just walk around, these limited social outings were highly treasured.

Just as I had experienced in previous situations, life can throw you curveballs. In my position as resident advisor, I observed an episode that has left a permanent mark on my life. Three weeks into the fall semester, a young man in my dorm received a poor grade on his first exam, prompting him to go up on the roof, stand on the edge and contemplate jumping. The man stood on the roof for hours as law enforcement tried to talk him down. There was a point when it seemed that they were successful, but the cruel encouragement of some residents of the building outweighed the efforts of law enforcement. The student just leaned over the side of the building and jumped to his death landing on the hard concrete below. In watching a student in my dorm commit suicide, I witnessed one of the saddest events of my life.

When I went home to the Smiths for Christmas, they told me that they decided to move their family to Ireland as they wanted a simpler life and to be more in touch with their Irish roots. While I understood and was happy for them in this decision, a part of me was scared. I was losing a major source of support and my connection to family. I also realized I was to be homeless once more. What little sense of security I had would soon vanish.

I was halfway through my sophomore year when I returned to Rutgers after Christmas break in the winter of 1985. I knew I would have nowhere to live once summer came. It was time again to start thinking ahead. Although the Smiths had given me a place to call home for six years, I suppose a part of me was always living in homeless mode. I have never had a place to call my own and always had the fear that I could lose the roof over my head at any time. This insecurity undoubtedly originated from the countless times we were forced to move once my parents divorced. I still remember my mother, siblings and I walking down the Better Hope public road at twilight when we thought the neighbors would be in bed carrying the few belongings we had on top of our heads. Those moves were some of the most embarrassing aspects of my life in Guyana and have consequently motivated me to be proactive in making sure I always have a roof over my head.

A friend of mine who was living in an off-campus apartment offered to sublet me a room for the summer. As I was able to secure a position as a summer camp counselor at the college, I now would have a source of income, so my housing problem was solved, or so I thought. I moved into the apartment at the start of the summer, but when the landlord came to collect the June rent and saw my race, he promptly kicked me out with a few choice words. This, of course, was not the first time I would be on the receiving end of those types of comments, but I did not think twice about those insults because I was just too busy or too focused on surviving to even care. I could not stay with Father Tom because I was taking summer classes and had my job on campus. As luck would have it, my course coordinator at school arranged for me to stay in my dorm room on the Rutgers' campus for the summer. It was a lonely summer as there was no meal plan and basically no one on campus except the janitorial staff. When I was not in class or at work, I spent most of my time riding my bike all over the deserted campus. I made do the best I could. As long as I could eat and had a roof over my head, I was content. I suppose that is the silver lining in not having much. I learned to be grateful for what I did have and not take anything for granted.

Before I knew it, fall of 1986 was upon me. I was going to be a junior at Rutgers. I was twenty-one-years-old. It has been six years since I left my father's house. The Smiths had moved to Ireland, but I would see Father Tom quite often. Once, we made a visit to Boston and stayed with his friend Brian. I remember this quite vividly as Father Tom got angry with me for not wanting to watch the movie *The Exorcist* because I was scared. This is one of the few times when he actually got mad at me. Father Tom literally did not say one word to me on the four-hour drive from Boston all the way back to New Brunswick all because he did not get to see that movie. I guess that disappointment shows he was human after all. We did, however, go together to see my second movie ever in the United States, *E.T. The Extra-Terrestrial.* I cried at the end of the movie as I suppose I related to E.T. on a personal level, always feeling like an outsider. Unlike E.T. however, I could not "phone home." There was no home to phone.

My junior year of college proved to be quite an unforgettable year. I had my job as a resident advisor, a girlfriend, and a declaration of a double major: Political Science and History. Father Tom continued to bestow much love and support on me as well. Upon my return to school from the summer, he bought me a car to help me be more independent and to make life a little easier. It was old, but it ran well. Despite the one time that three tires simultaneously blew out on the highway, I could not have been happier having my own means of transportation. My friends and I would pile into the car and head to New York

City to hang out over the weekends when we had free time. When we were studying, the car was quite an advantage. It helped us to make countless midnight rides for food runs. I loved having the independence and not relying on public transportation.

Father Tom also took me on my first vacation. We went to Puerto Rico over spring break and was I ever spoiled. Not only did we fly down with first-class tickets, we stayed at a five-star hotel. What an experience that was! Father Tom, along with his friends Brian and Michelle, had their daily scotch and water while I relaxed on a raft all day drinking those fancy drinks with an umbrella in it. At night for dinner, Father Tom treated me to the finest of restaurants. One restaurant served a buffet-style dinner. It was the first time I ever ate like that. Seeing all that food laid out for the taking was quite impressive. I never thought it was ever possible for life to be so fun. I savored every minute of that time in Puerto Rico.

Notwithstanding the memorable experiences and the happiness, I always seemed to worry that something was going to happen to undo the joy. This has always been a personality quirk of mine and remains so today. Perhaps it comes from living through so many ups and downs, but I am always hesitant to rely on the ups lasting for long. For example, despite my successful completion of coursework, I was never confident that I was really going to graduate. One night before finals while walking home from the library, I began to cry and pray that I would be able to actually get my diploma. My prayers were answered though, as my academic advisor informed me that I was eligible to graduate in June of that year, 1987. I was to be the first in my immediate family and second in my extended family to ever earn a bachelor's degree. This truly was the peak of happiness so far in my life.

I am not sure if it was for pride or the need for validation, but the week before graduation I went to find my biological father. It was now over six and a half years since I had seen or heard from him and I wanted to show him what the "loser" had done in the years since he had put me out. I had heard that he purchased a bar in Paterson. Some might more accurately refer to it as a strip club, and it was rumored that my father personally "interviewed" every dancer for her job at the bar. I drove to Paterson and when I walked into the bar, he was playing billiards. He did not change his focus or gaze as he was about to make his shot. Without saying a single word, I put a graduation ticket on the pool table and turned to exit. When I was almost out the door, I heard him call, "Gerry?" My father did not even recognize me after all those years. The boy he had abused seven years earlier had grown into a man and was about to graduate from college. I turned around and said, "Yes, and that is my graduation ticket on the pool table. I am graduating from Rutgers on Saturday." Surprisingly, my father showed up for the graduation ceremony beaming with pride while hand in hand with my step-mother. Any credit he believed he could take for this milestone is truly unfounded. It was Father Tom's hand which I shook after graduation and with whom I celebrated my hard-earned accomplishment. God is greater than any negative force mankind can create. Who God blesses, let no man curse.

CHAPTER 11

WHAT TO DO WITH A DEGREE?

"You have brains in your head. You have feet in your shoes.
You can steer yourself in any direction you choose.
You're on your own. And you know what you know.
You are the guy who'll decide where to go."

- Dr. Seuss

Things did not go well for Bob and Maureen in Ireland, so they moved back to the United Sates as a divorced couple. This so saddened me as I have seen first-hand the consequences of divorce. In my own experience, I have repeatedly seen how one party walks away due to his own selfish desires without giving thought to the impact of that decision on others. In the wake of that decision lies a destroyed family. It is especially the children who are hardest hit as they never recover from the tear in the fabric of their foundation. After the single unifying factor in their lives breaks in half, the children are then required to divide their love, their time and their connection to each parent individually.

I moved back in with Maureen and her children after graduation. It was a win-win as I not only appreciated having the warmth and support of Maureen's presence, but I was able to provide some assistance for Maureen by helping around the house with the chores that Bob usually took care of. I thought being a college graduate with a degree from Rutgers would make life easy, but it proved to be more difficult than I imagined. Upon returning to Maureen's, I could not find work. I even interviewed to sell kitchen knives, but being a salesman just was not for me. I was left with few options, so I wound up taking a job at a local chain restaurant waiting on tables until I could find a professional job. But, as I had done in the past, I took whatever work I could find until I could do better, so I set out to be the best server that restaurant ever had.

About one month after graduation I found work at a GED learning center. As life would have it, my father's latest girlfriend, Nala, was a student there. She often had to buy me lunch because I was always short on cash. Those were some lean years because I had purchased a new vehicle and I was helping Maureen with rent, so I did not have much left over for food. There were times I was in such need I had to ask my uncle for lunch money. I remember seeing my father picking up his girlfriend for lunch and taking her to a fast food restaurant across the street, yet I could not even afford a meal there. On occasion, because I was her teacher, Nala would give me a sandwich my father had bought her without his knowledge.

To earn some additional income, I secured a job at the local YMCA as a youth counselor. Although I thought this could only be beneficial, again, my plan and God's plan did not coincide. My first assignment was to serve as counselor for a lively, jovial, energetic young man, Andrew. He, too, was displaced by his family, so I really connected with him as he did with me. He emulated everything I did. One of my main responsibilities at the YMCA was to take children like Andrew away to a camp located on a lake in the wooded area of Wayne, New Jersey. We made that excursion several times through the year, so there was nothing unusual about the trip we were planning on this particular weekend. I picked up Andrew as I normally would, but this time his foster parents were not home and Andrew did not have his permission slip. He told me that he would have his foster parents drop the permission slip off at the YMCA. We loaded up the mini school bus with about fourteen teenagers and headed to the camp. At this point, I thought the permission slip was already taken care of. When we finally got to the camp, I directed the youngsters to go to their respective cabins in order to put their belongings away. Afterwards, we were all to meet up at the lake. It was a beautiful March day, still cold for springtime, but since the lake had already thawed we decided to take out the canoes. The plan was to paddle across the lake to the other side to check out a flock of Canadian geese that was nesting. While we were preparing everyone to make the trip, I learned that Andrew's permission slip never materialized. Despite my better judgment and my telling him that he could not go on the trip, I succumbed to Andrew's pleadings and ultimately allowed him to join us. This mistake was compounded by the fact that I realized we were one life jacket short, so I chose to go without one.

We all made our way across the lake with no problem. The campers were reveling in the fresh air and checking out the geese. At the end of this fun-filled day, when the sun began to go down, I instructed the campers to get back in the canoes to return to the other side of the lake. The water was cold and dark but in the spirit of continuing the jovial mood of the campers, I started to playfully splash water alongside the other two canoes. All of the boats were in close proximity to each other, so we all were laughing and enjoying the merriment. As we neared the shore, however, Andrew decided he did not want to be splashed anymore. Without any notice, he took off his life jacket, dove into the water and started swimming towards shore. He swam about 10 feet away and then turned around to look at me. I thought the odd expression on his face was one of his intending to play a joke on us. He went under the water and again, I thought he was just playing around. Andrew then came up above the water calling my name in panic. At this point I realized something was wrong, so I began to hastily paddle my canoe to the spot where Andrew was in the water. He continued to go under and then come back up to the surface, each time calling my name. I quickly stripped off the heavy brown leather jacket and sneakers that I was wearing. Looking at the water, all I could see were bubbles as Andrew had slipped under the water one last time. My superior swimming skills kicked in as I dove under the water searching for Andrew. Despite there being no visibility, I swam vigorously, even badly bruising my feet as I touched the bottom of the murky lake desperately looking for Andrew. I continued swimming to the shore, took off my sweat suit which, with the weight of the water, was weighing me down, and swam back to the spot where Andrew was last seen. I continued to search for Andrew in the freezing water, but to no avail. I despondently surfaced one more time, alone, seeing all of the campers in tears.

The next day, Andrew's lifeless body floated to the surface. I went to his funeral a few days later and I will never forget the image of his body and sad expression on his face as he laid in the coffin. I think of Andrew often, especially during late March and early April of every year.

Being relieved of my position with the YMCA, I was even more motivated to find a professional job in which I could use my higher education. I soon was able to secure a position as corporate analyst for an insurance company. Now I felt that my life could rightfully reflect the college degree which I had earned. I was now working in corporate America, making a nice salary and ready to kickstart a life I had envisioned for myself. With the substantial paycheck I was making, I could now afford to move into my own apartment and live the single life. My college girlfriend and I were no longer together since she moved to Florida. I was truly on my own. Father Tom and I went out to dinner often and spent much time together. I was learning how to mirror his alcoholic indulgences, but truth be told, I could never keep up. Although I went out often and dated, I soon came to realize that I truly missed my longtime college girlfriend.

Jasmine had graduated one year after I did and moved to Florida with her mother. We had dated through most of college and were figuring out if we were meant to be together for the long haul. Her move to Florida was supposed to help clarify what we meant to each other, and after a few months I realized I missed her greatly. I saw that as a sign that we should, in fact, get married. Once Father Tom gave his approval, and Jasmine agreed, wedding plans began and the last piece to my American dream life which I had envisioned was now in place.

My wedding to Jasmine, which took place in Harlem, reflected her Jamaican culture down to the reggae music and curried goat. Father Tom would never forgive me for being forced by my mother-in-law to taste the curried goat. For years after the wedding, he would speak of that meal, the extreme spiciness of the food and the distress in knowing it was an actual goat that he was eating. He would mimic the horns of a goat with his fingers as he described eating this endeared animal and feeling horrified with each mouthful.

The wedding was an intimate affair in the basement of Jasmine's family church. Despite the few extended family members who attended, no one from my immediate family was there. Although I had cordially invited my father to attend the wedding, he refused. Demonstrating another example of his own hypocrisy, my father had an issue with Jasmine's race. Despite the fact that my grandmother was one-hundred percent black, making my father half-black, he rejected Jasmine at every opportunity. For example, once, while we were dating, I took Jasmine with me to meet my father during one of my many attempts to reestablish a relationship with him. Upon entering the house, my father thunderously stomped himself downstairs, took one look at Jasmine, and marched himself back upstairs without a word.

The two of us turned into a family of three by the next year. My son was born, and we named Father Tom as his godfather. I was so nervous now to be a father. I even got chastised by Father Tom during the baptism for holding my son too high for the baptismal water to be sprinkled on him. I suppose I was really proud and wanted all to see my son. My version of the American dream was becoming a reality, allowing me to have so many hopes and dreams. Who would have thought that a homeless teenage immigrant could now have a college degree, a well-paying job, a wife and family?

SECTION III

FLORIDA

CHAPTER 12

MY CALLING REVEALED

"If God gives you something you can do,
why in God's name wouldn't you do it?"

- Stephen King

F ather Tom invited me over to see him once he learned of
my intention to relocate my family to Florida. It was the
winter of 1990. Jasmine wanted to be closer to her mother, and
I was very happy to exchange the cold dreary winters of the
Northeast for the tropical breezes, palm trees and year-round
warmth. I was also enthusiastic that our son would now have
the benefit of having additional family nearby and be able to
grow up with a grandmother. Plus, as I was able to transfer my
contract analyst job from the office in New Jersey to the one in
Florida, all the pieces seemed to be in place. Moving to Florida
was an exciting prospect, but I knew leaving Father Tom was
going to be difficult.

When I went to see Father Tom, he informed me that he
planned to leave me an inheritance when he passed. That took
me by surprise, but then what came next totally shocked me.
He offered to give me that inheritance before I moved to
Florida. As tears welled up in my eyes, I accepted the five-
thousand dollar offer which Jasmine and I ultimately used as a
down payment for a home. As priests take a vow of poverty,

and I saw how Father Tom lived and upheld his vows, I knew that five-thousand dollars was a huge outlay for him. First, it was Bob and Maureen who took me in as part of their family, giving me money to help me pay for my undergraduate tuition, and helping me achieve a foundation on which I could build my adult life. Now, it was Father Tom who was giving me financial support so that I could build upon that foundation and create an adult life for me and my family. I continue to be amazed by the fact that my own parents never gave a cent to help me, but it has been the kindness of strangers that has been instrumental in helping me advance.

Although I believed all the pieces which I needed to create this new adult life were falling into place, I did not count on the fact that the lateral transfer which was promised to me by my employer would not materialize as I was later told the position was filled. Without an income and needing to take care of my family, we decided to move in with my mother-in-law. The three of us lived in a single room in her home. Money was incredibly tight for months and many bills went unpaid. My car was repossessed, and I could not find work as hard as I tried. Although I had taught in a GED program back in New Jersey, I kept refusing to go back to teaching. I had grown accustomed to the professional "suit and tie" routine and felt a job in teaching would be a step backward since it would mean a huge pay cut. Nonetheless, when I could not make anything else happen, I fell back on my teaching experience and got a job as a substitute teacher. Upon walking into a classroom in what was considered one of the worst schools in the county, I felt an instant realization that this is where I was meant to be. I had found my calling. My twenty-eight year career as an educator began at that moment.

Walking into that classroom put me in a state of disbelief. The teacher who had been there prior to my starting had lost complete control of the classroom. She had allowed the students to make her so aggravated and push her to the limit that she had ended up throwing a book at one of them. The moment a teacher loses control, the students know that they are in charge and can then bring a teacher to ruin. These students had a plan. They continued to harass her in order to make the teacher reach her breaking point. Once that book was thrown, they knew they owned her. At that point they went to administration, claimed the teacher was being abusive and instigated her ultimate firing.

Classroom management is one of the most important elements in teaching. Without control over the students and classroom decorum, teaching is just not possible. Why would any student listen to instruction if they do not believe they have to? I have seen some very qualified and highly intelligent teachers lose their jobs early into their employment, not because they could not teach, but because they could not control their classroom. I have seen substitute teachers as well as new hires walk into a classroom and leave by the end of the day because they could not handle the students' behavior. I have witnessed teachers cowering in a corner of the classroom counting the seconds before security or administration would come to rescue them from out of control students. Personally, I too have borne the brunt of extremely abusive students who were looking to take control away from me. I have been called every name in the book. I have been threatened. I have been spat on. And, I have been challenged to fistfights. Although the type of behavior may vary depending on the type and location of a particular school, it is essential for any teacher to be a competent classroom manager in order to be successful.

This insolent behavior by which students attempt to take control is a far cry from a bygone era in education in which students were terrified to disrespect a teacher or, much worse, for a parent-teacher conference to be called. As a child growing up in Guyana, I could not even look at a teacher the wrong way. There was zero tolerance for any type of disobedience or disrespect. Any violation would result in three layers of beating before the end of the day: one from the teacher, one from the headmaster and one from the parent. In my case, I usually wound up with four beatings as I received an additional one from my grandmother, Tira the Terrible. As I walked along the only road in my village on my way home anticipating the beating I was to receive from my mother, I would have to pass my grandmother's house. Tira was always determined to have her turn in teaching me a lesson which she was very well-equipped to do. The level of beating which my grandmother inflicted set the bar for the one my mother would later deliver. She always felt as if she had to outdo whatever my grandmother did when it came to discipline. I never made it easy for her, however. I always made her catch me first.

I am not sure if it was the desire to meet the challenge, my strong belief in the value of education or just the fact that I needed a job, or a little of each of these factors. Either way, I knew that I was going to turn that classroom around. I lived on the streets of Jersey in some of the worst areas of the state. I knew these students' game plan as I had lived it and seen it many times before. Nothing was going to intimidate me as I was not about to lose a decent job after too many months of being unemployed. Somebody was going to have to give in that classroom and it was not going to be me. I met with the principal soon after my hiring about classroom management strategies and he had given me the go ahead to do whatever was necessary to get that classroom under control. I was ready.

Despite my body builder, two-hundred- and twenty-pound physique, those students were already planning how they were going to get rid of me. It did not take long before the first of the gang acted up. I wrote the first referral. As soon as that one was written, another of the gang acted up. Another referral was written. I wrote fifteen referrals in the span of thirty minutes. Security came and removed all of those students who were misbehaving at which point my class was half empty. Each one of those students who received a referral was suspended for three days. The next day was like a repeat of the day before. The students acted as if the previous referrals were never written and they continued to test me. They were not going to back down and they were determined to harass me in order to gain the control. One student really did challenge me to a physical confrontation. He asked me to step outside, which I did, although, in retrospect, I am not sure why. After calling me a few choice words, this student spit in my face. In Guyanese culture, spitting in one's face is the worst insult imaginable. Feeling that warm saliva running down my cheek, I almost lost my mind. I balled my hand into a fist and was seconds away from letting this student feel my fury. I managed to control that anger, however, and put my fist back into my pocket. Instead, I called for security, and when no one showed up to remove the student, I grabbed him by his backpack and marched him down to the principal's office myself. The next several days I continued to write referrals on that gang of mischief-makers until there were only three of them left. Word then spread that this new teacher was serious and not backing down from any confrontation. By the end of the first two weeks, I had that class in check. The substitute position for which I was hired quickly turned into a permanent position and so began my teaching career of almost three decades.

Few things in my life have brought me as much reward as being a teacher. This career is so far removed from what I intended for my life, but it has shaped me and brought me so much joy and gratification over the years. Although I had other aspirations, Father Tom, in his infinite wisdom, always said education would be the perfect profession for me. As my mother was a teacher, I wanted nothing to do with her profession when I was in Guyana. In a society where corporal punishment was acceptable until only a few years ago, my mother exercised that authority often. All of these years later,

I am still reminded by fellow classmates of the number of ears she twisted and fingers she smacked with the broad side of a ruler as she doled out discipline. I, embarrassingly enough, was her worst student. Whether it was just bad luck or her manipulations, I always wound up in my mother's class year after year. I was expected to be the model student because of her position as teacher and then headmistress, but I never lived up to that role. Consequently, I endured a daily beating from her. Who knew that I would wind up on the road that I tried so intently to avoid? Even more ironically, who knew that the profession which I never thought would be for me wound up being the most rewarding?

Although I never envisioned myself in the role of teacher, Father Tom was instrumental in instilling in me the understanding of the value of education. I learned back in my teenage years how fundamental education is to success. Beyond knowledge, education allows for options. The more education one has, the more options one has in life. I have learned that lesson first hand and constantly try to impart that idea onto my students. I seek to represent an example of the benefit of a higher education in order to inspire students. To demonstrate to students how my education has saved me through numerous obstacles helps to inspire in them the motivation to pursue their coursework. I use my own story to inspire my students on a daily basis. I relay to them my immigrant experience, my lack of knowledge of American ways, my lack of basics, my lack of resources and my minority status. In spite of the cards being stacked against me, I did what was needed to survive and to sustain a life on my own. During my early teenage years, I was not sure what I was going to do in order to create that life. But I knew, even back then, that education was the key. I strove for academic excellence, so I could get into a reputable college in order to pursue a more concrete goal once I determined where I wanted to fit in life. Education is the keystone to success and nothing makes me happier than to be part of the system which enables others to succeed as well. I truly found my calling.

CHAPTER 13

LOVE AND LOSS

"Ever has it been that love knows not its depth until the
hour of separation."

- Kahlil Gibran

For a number of reasons, most of which were my fault, my
marriage to Jasmine failed after five years. My family was
gone. Although I recognize my contributing role to the collapse
of my marriage, I did not have a solid understanding of what it
meant to be committed to another person and how to maintain
a family. How was I supposed to be a good husband and father
coming from the dysfunctional family that I did? My parents
certainly did not serve to be the role models of what to emulate
in order to maintain a successful marriage. That lack of a
positive example haunted me through two more failed
marriages and for what I expect will be for many years to come.
Consequently, I was on my own once again.

I was working full-time as a teacher in the public school
system and moved into a one-bedroom apartment to start over.
On one occasion when I was living alone, Father Tom came
down to spend the weekend with me and as we were out to
dinner with his friend Brian, he kept saying that his back was
hurting terribly. He could barely sit in the chair to eat. I
suggested he go and see a doctor on his return to New Jersey,
which he did. He called me a few days later to tell me that he

had cancer. The two packs a day of cigarette smoking had caught up to him. I was devastated and did not know what to do. This was the only father I had ever known. Father Tom told me he would be undergoing chemotherapy treatment, so I took time off from my job and flew up to New Jersey to be with him. My heart broke when I saw him. His hair had fallen out from the chemo. He was walking with a cane, and he had lost a ton of weight. This was the man that used to kick my butt in racquetball. Now he was as frail as an egg. I would take short walks with him around the rectory. He was stooped over and looked much older than his years. He would lean on me to help him walk and I could feel how much weight he had lost in his battle against cancer. I did my best to comfort him. I remained in New Jersey as long as I could, but eventually had to return to Florida.

The treatment Father Tom received initially was successful, so he retired to Arizona as a monsignor to be close to his brother Frank. I visited with him as often as I could. He had bought himself a beautiful townhouse almost across the street from his brother. The first time I walked into his home, I was genuinely moved as I saw that he had my picture hanging alongside that of his mother and father. He loved me as much as I loved him. At this point he was back to his jovial self and making his dry jokes as usual. I remember on my last visit to see him one Thanksgiving, I was one of about seventeen family members invited for holiday dinner. Father Tom knew how uncomfortable I felt being the lone brown face surrounded by all whites. In order to ease my discomfort, he blurted out his favorite line, "Hey, who let the black guy in?" He knew this would get me to laugh and it would break the tension I felt. Father Tom had done this so many times before that I knew his facial expression he made right before he would make this statement. Father Tom, Frank, and the rest of the family treated me with the deepest respect and love. They were all genuinely good-hearted people. They demonstrated the message that this world would truly be a better place if we could get beyond the racial differences that divide us. All of humanity is made in God's image and if we all could remember that, we would focus on the things that unite us which would allow us to see the good in everyone. Dear Father Tom, it has taken me a while to get it right, but I have finally gotten it together, in a large part because of you.

Soon after, I met and fell in love with the woman who would become my second wife. I saw her from behind in a local coffee shop and vowed that if her front matched her back, I was going to pursue her. Not only was Gaby as beautiful on the outside, but her inner beauty shone even brighter. Her personality, morals, work ethic and loyalty to family were exemplary. She was fun, creative and a loving mother to her daughter and my son. She was a wonderful woman and treated me with the utmost respect and unrivaled love. Ironically, her family disapproved of me because of my race just as my father disapproved of my first wife, but Gaby continued to stick be my side as I tried to build a life for us. God knows, she was the one I should have stayed with. I was determined to get it right this time, but the same old demons came back to haunt me. They came storming back into my life with a tried and true formula, an attractive woman. Try as I might to avoid temptation, it was futile. I allowed another person into my life and it ended up destroying my marriage and family. I truly loved Gaby but was not able to be the type of husband she deserved. Knowing that I was the cause of her hurt, I quickly left Gaby's life, so I would not cause her any more pain. Consequently, I was never able to let her know how sorry I was for messing up our marriage, that it was all my fault, and for that I take full responsibility.

My heart was broken over losing Gaby, so I decided that maybe I was meant to be alone. I visited with Father Tom often over those years and we talked frequently over the phone. I knew that he was still sneaking cigarettes on the side. When I would visit with him, he would disappear for a few minutes and come back in and I could smell the cigarette smoke on him.

Even when he was in recovery from cancer treatment, as disciplined as this man of God was, he could not control the nicotine addiction that would eventually lead to cancer ravishing his body and to his eventual death. The collapse of my second marriage combined with the knowledge that this addiction was at some point going to take Father Tom away from me, made me realize that I would be alone. In order to protect myself I felt that I needed to build walls around my heart and not allow myself to become entrenched in a serious relationship. I was determined not to marry another time as I was never going to allow myself to experience that unbearable pain of loss again.

CHAPTER 14

NEVER SAY NEVER

"The course of true love never did run smooth."

- William Shakespeare

In the fall of 2002, I went home to Guyana with my girlfriend at the time. Although she was a nice woman, I knew the relationship had no future as I had sworn I would never marry again. I had decided that I would not allow myself to love anymore and would just accept whatever non-serious relationship came into my life. Yvette and I got along well and that was enough for me. She was good to me, but I thought, after having two failed marriages, I should not make that commitment again. I knew this bothered her because she eventually wanted to get married.

Upon arriving in Guyana, I met with my mother who I had not seen since her last trip to the United States five years earlier, and we had a fairly good time together. She liked Yvette but agreed with me that she was not right for marriage. My mother still had hopes for me to marry again as I was relatively young, and she felt I would be happier with someone in my life, someone to take care of me. She said that I needed to get married to someone from my own culture. Someone who understood my ways and could relate to who I was. She had someone in mind for me. She told me that she would arrange for me to meet her in church the Sunday before I was scheduled to fly back to the United States. I did not know who this person was, but it did not matter to me as I was not really interested in meeting her. My mother made a convincing argument, however, so I reconsidered my decision. I decided I should listen to her for once in my life and honor her wishes. I did not know why as a grown man at my age I felt the need to comply. I certainly over the years rarely did. Maybe I was just tired. Maybe I felt that she had better insight into women than I did. Anyway, I went to church with her to meet my potential future wife.

When I went to church with my mother, I felt like a foreigner. I had not been back to Guyana in thirteen years and so I did not know many of the people in the congregation. As I walked into church with my mother, I received many curious stares. As much as I knew no one there, no one there knew me either. I did, however, notice the name of a Natalya Lawrie as one of the readers for that day's mass. Assuming that she was related, I was curious about her. My mother, affirming my assumption, promised to introduce me to her at the end of the service. She is my third cousin on my father's side. I had first left Guyana even before she was born.

As I sat in the front pew of the church, my mom's favorite seat in the church, I started to look around to try to figure out who the person was that I was supposed to meet and potentially marry. All I knew about her was that her name was Ana. I could not figure out who she was, but as I scanned the congregation, there was a young white woman sitting in the back of the church. That was a very strange sight in light of the fact that ninety-nine percent of the Guyanese population is of either Indian or African origin. Every time I stared to look back at her, she was looking at me. Although I found myself attracted to her, I told myself I had a purpose for being there and she was not it. I was there to meet the woman my mother had chosen for me.

At the end of the service my mother said she would take me to meet Ana who was present in church, but would first introduce me to my cousin, Natalya. She then began walking me towards the beautiful Anglo girl who had been sitting in the back of the church. She introduced Natalya to me as my great uncle Lolo's granddaughter. The same uncle I used to carry soup for as a child when he was sick. The same one I used to care for towards the end of his life. The same uncle I used to clean up after when he would soil himself. The same uncle whose funeral I witnessed from the time they bathed him, to the making of his coffin, and to his eventual burial in the family plot. Now learning that this beautiful girl with whom I had been exchanging stares during the church service was related to me, I was disappointed. I killed the attraction in my heart. My mother then took me to meet Ana, a nice enough young lady, but I had no feelings towards her.

I enjoyed the rest of my stay in Guyana. Since my mother's idea of connecting me with Ana did not pan out, I focused on Yvette and ignored the many other suitors who made their interest known. The day before I left to return to the United States, I stopped by the pharmacy where Natalya worked. It was located across from my mother's house, which made it easy to drop in to say goodbye to her. We chatted for a few moments and I gave her my home address so that we could stay in touch. At this point the fact that she was family overshadowed any of the initial attraction I felt. I came back to the States and proceeded with my life.

Approximately three weeks after I returned to the States, I received a letter from Natalya. In the letter she told me about herself, how we were related and about life in Guyana. Natalya was from the poor side of the family, or as her aunt and my cousin referred to it, the "low Lawries." All aspects of life were tough for her in Guyana. What Americans would call basic necessities would not only be considered luxuries but also items that would be inconceivable for her to ever have. I wrote Natalya back and exchanged e-mail addresses and phone numbers so that we could communicate quicker as letters took forever.

Natalya and I started communicating in June of 2002. Our conversation started out as two cousins who never knew each other and were catching up on their history. Two months into our communication, we both realized that we were attracted to each other; at least I was attracted to her. She claimed she was attracted to me; however, I am now convinced those professed feelings were all a sham, spoken all in the name of using me as a ticket out of Guyana. As I look back and can see more clearly how the dots connected, I am certain the love was one-sided. Hindsight is twenty-twenty, but at the time I allowed my love to color any doubts about her words. We therefore made the decision to break all the established norms of society and start a relationship.

Over the next few months, I realized that I could no longer stay with Yvette. She was very upset when I ended the relationship, but my love for Natalya continued to grow. Despite my initial belief that I would never love again, my heart had something different to say. My mother's words continued to ring in my head that perhaps this love would be different since it was with someone of my own culture and heritage. Despite her lack of resources and understanding of the world, she knew my ways and culture was something we shared. I did not have that tie with my previous two wives. By October of 2002, despite our genealogical connection, Natalya and I decided to get married. The fact that we shared blood and kin was an added bond for us though we were sure the rest of the family would not see it that way. We planned on exchanging our vows during Christmas break of that year, but we did not let anyone know of the plan as we decided to avoid the disapproval of our family for as long as we could.

Natalya and I agreed to inform our parents of the intended nuptials when I would arrive in Guyana in December. At the start of my Christmas break from work, I flew home to Guyana. Natalya met me at the airport. It was awkward at first, but we soon warmed up to each other. We were careful on the streets and kept a safe distance from each other in order not to create suspicion as to our feelings for each other or our intentions. Now I understand the awkwardness and the reason for the distance between us. I often teased her about it, but she always laughed it off as a joke. In retrospect, Natalya's self-imposed distance and apparent awkwardness was not reflective of her protecting our relationship but rather it was a display of the reality of her lack of feelings for me. Her not wanting to be near me was not about her love for me, but my ability to provide a ticket out of Guyana for her.

We traveled together to the coast and then split from each other at a certain point to avoid suspicion because of the nosey nature of our community. My mother was shocked to see me back at her house so soon. She had seen me once in seventeen years and then I showed up twice in less than a year, so naturally she was suspicious. I knew informing her of my plans would not be easy. No sooner had I put down my luggage, my mother laid in on me with the series of questions beginning with, "How come you are back so soon?" I knew she could not beat me now as she used to, because I was a grown man, so I faced my fears and told her my true reason for being in Guyana: to marry Natalya. She took it better than I thought but was predictable in her response. After telling me that she would be very embarrassed because of the familial connection as well as the lowly status of Natalya's part of the family, she then proceeded to ask me a hundred questions: "Did Natalya know I had a child?" "Was Natalya aware of my age?" Finally, her last question was, "Did Michael know and give his approval?" I told her I would be meeting with Natalya's father the following day and would ask for her hand in marriage at that time. My mother then informed me that if Michael would give his approval, she would give hers as well.

It was not going to be easy to ask Natalya's dad for his permission to marry his daughter. Natalya's father, Michael, was my father's first cousin and thus my second cousin whom I had never met. I experienced genuine fear for the first time ever. I knew Michael's father, my uncle Lolo, as a little boy. He was my grandfather's brother. Uncle Lolo was a hell-raiser and died a very sad death. His children abandoned him in death as he had abandoned them in life. None of his children were at his funeral. I was age 10 when he died, and so I never knew he had children, although I had heard he had a son named Michael. Who would have imagined that that same Michael was soon to be my father-in-law? Now here I was, because Natalya insisted it was the proper thing to do, mustering the courage to ask Michael to marry his daughter: a man I had never met in my life, my father's first cousin.

Natalya lived in a modest house made of wood which sat on the banks of the Pomeroon River. It was a two story structure with the downstairs portion at that time being used as a storage area. Later that portion would be converted into an apartment which was rented out. Although considered modest by Guyanese standards, I saw it to be one of the most beautiful and serene places I had ever seen. In the back of the house Michael grew many fruits and vegetables. Trees and plants from which they grew oranges, cashews, mangoes, peppers, yucca, plantains, avocado and pears abounded the back of Natalya's family home. Often one could see flocks of parrots come to gorge themselves on this wide assortment of fruits and vegetables. I will always remember this little piece of natural paradise that stood behind Natalya's home.

The arrangement Natalya and I made was that she would inform her dad of our intent. Therefore, when I arrived at their house to speak with Michael, it would be a mere formality. This, however, was very far from the reality of the situation. When I got to her house, I saw Natalya smiling and I quickly gestured to her, asking whether she had spoken to her father. When she said no, I started to sweat. I was meeting my cousin Michael for the first time in my life and I was asking for his daughter's hand in marriage.

Michael was very happy to see me because even though he knew my mother had a son, he had never met me as I had left Guyana many years before. Michael could not have been more welcoming. He brought out the customary rum to drink and a spread of garlic pork along with holiday sponge cake. We talked about the family and I am sure he was pleased to have me visit with him since I was considered one of the "high Lawries." As warm as he was, I was quickly losing the courage to ask for his permission for Natalya's hand in marriage, and Natalya refused to help. My time in Guyana was limited and plans were already in place for the marriage, so I knew I had to find a way to do it. I drank more rum in order to feel more confident and then I finally asked the question. Michael was initially in shock, but then he started to ponder what I had just proposed.

Michael started to trace how far apart Natalya and I were as cousins and we came to the conclusion that we were third cousins. He then asked Natalya if she loved me, to which she stated yes, and then he asked what my mother's response was to the idea. I told him her response was contingent upon his answer. He assented, so Natalya and I were married a few days later. A day after our marriage I flew back to the United States and immediately filed the necessary papers for Natalya to leave Guyana. I was told by the immigration authorities that she would have to wait about one year in order to join me in the United States. We decided to endure the separation, so we could have a better life in the United States.

CHAPTER 15

SACRIFICES

"True love is selfless. It is prepared to sacrifice."

- Sadhu Vaswani

I started to lay a foundation for the life I planned to build with Natalya. I picked up extra hours at a second job in anticipation of her arrival by year's end. I was now teaching in a public school during the day and a high school GED program at night, saving as much money as I could. We talked a lot over the phone about the life we would build together. I went down to Guyana over my spring break from school and then again that summer. After I came back to the United States at the end of that summer visit, Natalya informed me that she was pregnant. Looking at the dates on the calendar, I realized my child would be born in the United States. I was overjoyed to think he would be a natural born citizen.

In October of that next year, when Natalya was supposed to join me in the United States, I called the immigration office and was informed that the wait for her to immigrate would be another three years. I was devastated as that news translated into four years apart from my wife and new child. I could barely stand to be apart from my wife for one day, much less years and was afraid that my marriage would collapse if I had to wait that long. So, I made one of the hardest decisions of my life: I decided that after living for twenty-six years in the United

States, I would move back to Guyana to be with my wife and child. Looking back, I should have given that decision some additional thought as the time I would spend in Guyana would be one of the most difficult I have ever endured. I was painfully made aware of why my mother so many years earlier had struggled so hard to get me and my sisters out of Guyana.

I sold everything I owned to raise as much cash as possible: my house, motorcycle and luxury car. Additionally, I cashed in my pension from the school board. Ultimately, I amassed one-hundred and twenty-nine thousand dollars and was eager to move. My driving force was my desire to build a life with Natalya and my son: to create a home life and family that I never had myself. Notwithstanding the fact that I had lived in the United States for over twenty-six years and was so removed from the culture, psyche and politics of Guyana, I was determined to make it back "home" all for the sake of family.

Without having a specific direction in mind for how to provide for my family, my father-in-law suggested I get into the gold mining business as a main source of income. As a secondary source of income, one that would be more reliable and consistent, he suggested I ferry passengers by boat to an area known as the Northwest District. This four-hour journey through the open sea would shuttle people from my hometown of Charity to Port Kaituma. As the Northwest District was also the main mining area in Guyana, I could also carry miners and their equipment by boat.

With a plan in place, I bought most of the mining equipment in Guyana and some in the United States and then set in motion the mining operations. Concurrently, I purchased a boat and engine to establish the ferry business. I also set aside a bit of money to build a little house for my family. It seemed the plans for the dredge were proceeding as scheduled. However, soon my father-in-law and I had a terrible disagreement and he withdrew his support from the project. We had a blow-out confrontation and even after his knowing that I had invested every dime I had ever earned and was completely in debt, my father-in-law kicked me out of his house. I was so angry that night of our argument, I wound up swimming across the Pomeroon River in the middle of the night to get to the mainland.

The Pomeroon is a beautiful river. It serves the residents who live alongside it in many ways. It is a water highway to most of the mining districts in Guyana as well as the means of transportation for the local people to get from their homes on the river to the coastal areas where they can conduct business. However, there is a dark and eerie side to that same river. After nightfall there is no way to the main road. There are no lights on the river and it becomes pitch black at night. In addition to the piranha living under the surface, there is an extremely strong current. There is a fierce downward pull as the tide recedes out to sea and carries the river water with it to the access point of the river. I have seen and known many people who have lost their lives on that river.

The night of the argument, Michael began to quarrel with me. To this day, I am not sure why he picked this fight. All I know was that I was not in a state of mind to engage in such a confrontation. My entire life's earnings were tied up in the mining investment and I needed to be able to get along with Michael as he was not only my father-in-law, but he was my partner. Whatever issues he was arguing over were petty at the time and totally blown out of proportion considering the magnitude and importance of this business venture. His barrage of insults brought me to my tipping point at which time I dove into the water to escape his badgering. I have always been a strong swimmer, but there have been many other strong swimmers who could not withstand the force of the water's current. I knew I was being swept downriver, but I also knew I had to get across. I held my head above the frigid, black water and swam with all my strength to the mangrove roots I saw ahead of me. As I made it across to the other side, I held steadfastly onto the mangrove roots. My entire body was still relatively soft from the easy physical life I had as a teacher, and so I took a beating as I pulled along the roots to get to the shore and river dam. My feet and body were badly bruised and mangled from making my way through the prickly roots, but with a Herculean effort, I made my way to the other side of the river. I was wet, cold, and scratched all over my body as I tried to find the access road to the coastal area of my hometown of Charity where I could find a place for my family to stay.

Despite Michael's withdrawal from the project, my brother-in-law ultimately agreed to help me. We arranged to alternate the management of the mining operations and the operation of the ferry between the two of us. We would switch responsibilities periodically. By having both endeavors covered, we could keep the employees from robbing us blind as someone always had to be in place to oversee the daily operations. Sadly, this is a reality within Guyanese society. No matter what the relation, theft is a constant concern as people seek to pursue the material possessions they desire. The disparity between rich and poor in Guyana is heartbreaking. The wealthy, a small minority of the population, live quite the luxurious life: driving the fanciest of vehicles, wearing the most beautiful designer clothing and living in homes that rival some in the United States. However, the majority of the population lives in stark contrast. Most of Guyanese society live in squalor, getting by from day to day and meal to meal. This reality truly validates the statistic that more Guyanese actually live outside of Guyana. Most try to leave in the hopes of a better life, just as my mother had hoped for me.

For two weeks I prepped the equipment for the dredge and then hired eight workmen to join the crew. Late one afternoon in June, we were ready to leave and make our way to the Northwest District. I hated leaving my wife and young son as I would be gone for two to three months deep into the heart of the Guyana rain forest to look for gold, but this was the plan we had settled on so that I could provide for my family. I believed that my hard years struggling to survive in the United States would help prepare me for what I thought I would need to endure to get my business started.

After sailing down the Pomeroon that afternoon, we travelled all night with the mining equipment and enough supplies to sustain everyone for two months. I laid out in the open boat on a sack of rice with a tarp wrapped around me to protect me from the sea spray. The salt water showered me the entire night as we made our way on the all-night journey to the Northwest District. We made it into Port Kaituma late afternoon on the next day and unloaded the equipment. We set up a base camp and, as I stayed at camp to protect the equipment and supplies, the rest of my crew went into town to drink and chase women. Knowing my men would probably not be seeing another woman for the next three months, I understood they would be lonely and desirous of female companionship.

There was, however, the possibility of cavorting with prostitutes, most of whom came over from bordering Brazil with the intent of making a quick dollar off a miner. This socialization would take place in the "cayamus": a hurriedly built shack where there would be music and over-priced beer. These women for hire were not of the best quality, but a miner who had been away from women would certainly be satisfied. Unfortunately, many men would end up spending all of their money on these women. Pay that should have gone to their families. Men oftentimes would work a full three months to earn money for their families and then blow it all in one night with one of these prostitutes. Miners often engaged in drunken brawls over these women, sometimes becoming maimed, disfigured or even dead.

Sometime past midnight at our first camp base, I was roughly awakened by a gun to my head. This was the second time a gun would be held to my head, only this time it was not by criminals. It was a Guyanese police officer who had come to check on the ownership of all the mining equipment. I was able to show them that the equipment was registered and that I had receipts for all of it. Everything I owned was sitting on that embankment which represented twenty-six years of sacrifice and hard work toiled in the United States. I was going to do whatever was necessary to protect it.

At 6 a.m. the next morning, we left Port Kaituma, an area most infamous for being the site of the Jonestown mass suicide. I hired an army truck and drove to a place called Eyelash—a backcountry mining area where we could buy supplies before heading out to the worksite. We spent the next two and a half weeks there as we searched for a permanent worksite to set up our equipment. We walked for what seemed like hundreds of miles. We walked so much that the soles of my feet became infected from wearing wet, high rubber boots for so long. I could not put my feet down for days. We ultimately located a suitable worksite and began the arduous task of moving the equipment and setting it up in place. Everything had to be manually taken to the worksite, which was approximately eight miles through the jungle. Two, six-cylinder diesel engines had to be pulled by teams of men through the thick jungle. This was back-breaking work to say the least. As this venture was my responsibility, I did everything my men did and most times was at the lead pulling those heavy engines through the jungle. I had never worked that hard in my life. It took us a week to move the equipment to the dredging site in the middle of the jungle. At the end of each day, every single muscle in my body ached; however, I would wake up every morning and do it all over again.

After a few weeks of this back-breaking work, I adjusted to the regimen of all the manual labor that was involved in gold mining. Gold mining is an extremely competitive business. I knew it was going to be difficult to be successful as an outsider coming into the business without connections as it was the government that had the power and control over the system. Most small business owners, such as I was at the time, were usually dependent on working on someone else's land and giving the owner a percentage of profit. The problem with that system, however, was that after the miner had spent thousands of dollars getting equipment to the worksite and gold was discovered, the owner of the land would either ask for a higher percentage or kick the miner off his land. Sometimes the owner might even bring in his own equipment and surround the miner to squeeze him out. Additionally, most of the major gold producing lands were in the hands of a few oligarchs with strong connections to the government. These connections would be used for personal or illegal gain. For example, I would not be surprised if a large number of miners were actually using the mining business as a cover to illicitly move drugs out of the country. After all, Guyana is a popular shipping point for cocaine entering the United States and possibly Europe. Guyanese are a creative people and find all kinds of ways to try to get "the white lady" out of the country.

This foray began my new career as a gold-miner and boat operator. We worked in the jungle from sunrise to sunset. The only sound heard during the day was the constant humming of the diesel engines and the gushing of water as it propelled away from the jets to cut away the soil. We worked like demons in the open mining pit, cutting away the topsoil with the water jets to get to the gravel some six feet down in which, if we were lucky, the gold lay. Our appetites matched the intensity of our work, so the cook had his work cut out for him. He prepared our meals over an open fire in order to satisfy the hunger of the entire crew. After the daily recordings of country western music ended, at night the only sound that could be heard were the crickets, frogs and the jaguars hunting for food. My men and I slept outdoors in hammocks under tarpaulin tents. It took a little time to re-master the art of sleeping in hammocks due to the constant motion, but the daily vigor created a greater need for rest.

Our first wash-down or processing for gold was very promising. We scored five ounces in three days, which was the equivalent of five thousand U.S. dollars. I was very hopeful. If this income continued, it would provide a nice life in Guyana for me and my family and would supplement whatever income the boat generated. For the next month and a half, however, we mined little or nothing from the work site. Without reaping any additional revenue, I still had to provide meals for the ten men in the camp and cover all other operational expenses. My hopes of running a successful business and providing a nice life for my family in Guyana were beginning to fade.

To add to this dismal outlook, I ran out of drinking water and was forced to start drinking the creek water that the men consumed in camp. That, however, was a terrible mistake as my body had become accustomed to the clean water in the United States. I had lost all immunity I had developed to this type of water from my younger days in Guyana. Consuming this water resulted in my contracting typhoid. To complicate matters, despite using a mosquito net, I was bitten by the dreaded malaria-bearing mosquito. Shortly thereafter, I contracted malaria as is a common occupational hazard of miners. I became so sick I could not lift myself out of the hammock to urinate. Nothing stayed in my stomach. It was as if food was an alien substance to my body, and I dropped close to ten pounds a week. Between the extreme weakness and reading the facial expressions of my men, I knew that if I did not get out of the camp to the waterfront and ultimately to the local health center, I would die. My brother-in-law, along with the help of the entire crew, carried me on a stretcher walking six miles from the camp to the main road out of the jungle. He had used our only source of communication, a radio set, and sought medical assistance. Once on the main road, the men got me to a waiting pickup truck whose driver was to get me to the local medic. At this point I was so weak, I could no longer walk.

The medic was based at the local hospital located in Port Kaituma. I was so sick that to this day I can barely recall the events of that ride to Port Kaituma, a thirty mile ride through some of the worst roads on earth. The trip to the hospital took about five hours. Once at the health center, I was immediately put on intravenous fluids. A plane was ordered to bring me to Georgetown because the medic on site at the health center thought I would die without the proper treatment. The treatment I needed was not available at this local health center, which was located so far from civilization. This medical facility, and I use that term loosely, had such limited resources, all the medic could do was try to keep me alive until I could be transported. It was a nightmare during those days while I waited to be evacuated. The facility was poorly lit so there was always a depressing din hovering over. Despite the fact that my bed was covered with a mosquito net, that net was totally tattered. The countless holes allowed entry for an overabundance of mosquitoes which swarmed the area and provided access to all parts of my body. The same mosquitoes which got me sick now had additional opportunities to continually bite me. Food was as scarce as the medical resources. I will never forget the kindness of a young lady named Liz who brought me food while I remained at the health center. I was entirely grateful for that nourishment since it was not provided for by the hospital. Without it, for sure, I would not have made it. This is another example of a stranger's act of kindness. But for the grace of God I managed to hold steady until the chartered plane finally arrived to transport me.

Three days later, I was flown into the capital city, Georgetown, to the only functional public hospital that was able to treat me. I laid in bed for over a week, sick as a dog, and feeling as if I were at death's door. The man on the cot next to me was infected with the same malaria I had. His complexion was almost blue, and his body looked more like a skeleton than a man. He died the same night I got there, which added to my genuine concern for my own situation. At one point, I remember being so weak that I almost collapsed on the way to the bathroom. I ultimately was discharged from the hospital and sent back home to Charity where my family lived. I was blessed to be able to spend quality time with them, and I eventually fully recovered.

While I convalesced at home back to health, my business was quickly collapsing at the worksite. My brother-in-law did all he could to help sustain the business, but the gold was just not there. The prospector had done a poor job of evaluating the site. In the meantime, the passenger boat was doing terribly because the competition for passengers was fierce and the operator of my boat was helping himself to the income being generated by the boat while I was sick and away from the operations. The hopes I had for a successful business to provide for my family again began to look very dim.

After about three weeks, I felt well enough to go back to work, so I headed out to the dredge. There was still no gold to be found. When I switched responsibilities with my brother-in-law and started work on the boat, it was no better. There were many nights I ended up sleeping on the bottom of my open boat on the Kaituma River because I could not afford a hotel room for the night. The number of paying passengers I was able to ferry had greatly declined due to the competition, as did my income. There were many meals missed during those difficult days waiting for passengers. Whatever little money I had, I saved in order to make sure I had enough to get home to my family. It was baffling to me that as a business owner, I did not even have enough money to eat. I remember begging a man for a cup of coffee and a roll to eat after riding all night on the hot engine of an excavator making its way to the waterfront in order to save money to get home. My entire investment and life earnings were going under and no matter what I tried, there was nothing I could do to stem the bleeding.

As the physical and emotional sacrifices compounded, I returned from my third trip to the mine site and apprised my wife of the situation. We came to the indisputable conclusion that the business was not working and there was nothing that could be done to improve it. At this point I was getting help with food and money from whatever source was available just to live. It was unbelievable that just a few months earlier I had arrived in Guyana with over one hundred and twenty-five thousand dollars, and now I was at the point where I could barely afford to eat. I had to do something drastic. I had to change our circumstance.

CHAPTER 16

DRASTIC

"Desperate Times Call for Desperate Measures"
- proverb

I still had not heard from the U.S. embassy at this time and realized we had to get out of Guyana in order to create some sort of life for ourselves. We decided we would go to the United States embassy and ask again for permission for my family to migrate to the U.S. Again, the answer remained no. I was so desperate, I resorted to one of the few ways a person can get out of Guyana: a method known as "backtrack." It requires payment of thousands of dollars to smugglers in order to get a person out of Guyana illegally. At this point, I was willing to do anything to emigrate, so I sold our house and motorcycle to raise the money. I paid half the fee upfront and was supposed to pay the other half upon my wife's arrival in the United States. She was supposed to come via Jamaica and then, through unknown sources there, she would be granted a visa and passport to come to the United States. We were instructed to dress in specific clothing, so the smugglers would recognize us. We got all the way to Jamaica. The plan was to pick us up and provide an exit visa to the U.S. At the airport we were greeted by a group of men who took us to a shady hotel. I was carrying the remaining portion of the payment owed, which amounted to eight thousand dollars. Carrying this bundle of cash caused me genuine concern as I did not know who these men were and with whom they were associated. We arrived at the hotel and then learned that the process, which was supposed to take only two days, was now to turn into a week. The men suggested that I leave my wife with them while they complete the process and I should go on to the States myself to wait for her. Of course, I would not leave Natalya with complete strangers, especially these questionable ones. For the whole time we were there, we were interacting with shady characters. It was like reenacting a spy movie as we were told to change cars on several occasions because we were unsure if we were being followed. Carrying large sums of cash which represented final payment for the desired visa in addition to not knowing who I could trust made the whole experience quite frightening. This uneasiness, combined with the fact that I could not stay in Jamaica that long while leaving Natalya alone with these dubious characters, forced us to make the decision to go back home to Guyana. This was a wise decision in retrospect as we did not break any American laws which could have impacted my family's ability to enter the United States legally at a later time.

When we returned to Guyana, it was the same situation as before we left: no money, no food, and no income being generated by the business. As the months went by, we became more and more desperate, so we decided to try to self-sponsor to any western country that would have us. We began this strategy by approaching the Canadian embassy—with no luck. However, a short distance away from the American embassy was the British embassy, so we decided to inquire there. The diplomat informed us that if we had an address in the United Kingdom and someone there willing to accept us, Britain would grant us an ancestral visa. By establishing that my great-grandfather was from Scotland and managing to track down a long-lost cousin who agreed to accept us in the United

Kingdom, our visas were finally now going to materialize. I sold the boat and the dredge and put together as much money as I could and then immigrated to England with my family. I had no job, no source of income, a one-year-old baby and was now going to stay with someone I had not seen in twenty-six years.

At this point I had lost all contact with my dear friend Father Tom. I thought about him often, but I did not have nor could I get current contact information for him. I had no way of connecting with him. I was no longer a young boy who could run to him when things got tough. I had to solve this problem, and the many others to come on my own.

So, on a beautiful sunlit afternoon in the summer of 2003, we left Guyana on a one way trip to England. With my beautiful wife and young son, I finally had my family together. We landed at Heathrow airport full of anticipation for a promising future.

Life in England with my cousin Derek was much harder than we expected. I went looking for jobs daily. My wife cooked and cleaned Derek's apartment to pay for our keep until I could find employment, but a job never materialized. Without work, we never had a dime to spare. The only treat we ever allowed ourselves to indulge in was an occasional soda that we would share. We tried to eat a meal and a half a day so as not to be a burden on our host. Derek, however, never returned that courtesy. He drank heavily and was terribly abusive to us when he became drunk, especially to me because he knew we were dependent on him. He would wake me up at all hours of the night to go and buy him beer and cigarettes and would play with my one-year-old son in a very rough manner that could have potentially hurt him. Often, he would swing my son by his arms in his drunken state. A beautiful gold, pricey bracelet that was given to my son as a customary gift at birth, mysteriously disappeared while living in England with Derek. I sucked up my pride and endured all these abuses in order to give my family a better life.

After four months in England, not being able to find a job and not being able to support my family, I knew I had to do something. I had no place in America to which I could go. I had no relationship with my father and I did not know where Father Tom or my sisters were. The only place I could think of to go for help was my former church in Florida. I called the church and explained my situation. I was put in contact with a parishioner who agreed to find me a job and place to stay if I could make my way back to the States. With tears streaming down my face and a completely broken heart, I left my beautiful wife and one-year-old son once again and headed back to the United States. I arrived at the Ft. Lauderdale airport with five dollars in my pocket. I met Bradley, the gentleman who agreed to sponsor me at an extended stay hotel that he had arranged for me. I immediately began working for him, sweeping his warehouse or whatever other work he wanted me to do. Knowing I was a college graduate, I could not allow pride to derail my motivation to provide for my family, even if it meant having to sweep floors. I have always ascribed to the philosophy that one must do what he must until he can do better. Any job is better than no job. In the meantime, my wife was back in England with no money, not even to buy diapers for our son. Bradley gave me a hundred dollars to send to Natalya only after I broke down and cried my eyes out to him explaining why I needed the money. How can I ever forget these things? I know I cannot, and I pray that my children will learn of the sacrifices made for the sake of family.

Bradley did not have a legitimate company. He ran an illegal boiler room operation where he created a phony company that sold nitrogen powered engines as a cleaner alternative source to diesel and gas powered engines. The people who worked for Bradley sat in offices all day throughout the week and made phone calls to people across the globe pushing his scheme. Shockingly, there were people who did invest. On Sundays,

Bradley went to church. I suppose Bradley had hoped to use me in some capacity to generate income for his company. He soon realized I would not fulfill that need, so he let me go. I was never a successful salesman when I had a real product to sell, much less without a real one. Although I was grateful to Bradley for giving me an opportunity to plant roots back in the United States at a time when I needed that chance, I now had no job, no place to stay, and was back to square one.

I prayed and asked God for guidance. On a hunch, I called an old friend of mine who was then a principal at a middle school and asked her if she had any positions available. She said there were none available as a full-time teacher but that she would take me on as a sub. When a full time position became available she promised that she would hire me. Additionally, I contacted an old friend I worked with at my former school and she agreed to let me sleep on her sofa until I could get back on my feet. I stayed with Ms. Brown for close to eight months.

Ms. Brown is one of the most God-fearing people I know. She took me in and gave me emotional and spiritual guidance with the mindset that caring for another is what God would expect of her. She even went as far as to try to expel the demons she became convinced that lived inside me. My life thus far had been so difficult, for her there was no other explanation except that a demon or curse infiltrated my being. So, on a prearranged date, Ms. Brown and her church sister had me stand in the middle of the living room while the two women began to speak in tongues. This activity is a sight to behold as I became witness to these women losing control over their bodies as they became overcome by the holy spirit. Their physical actions were basically taken over by God as they became the vessels through which God can do His work. Ms. Brown and her church sister began praying in tongues. This began in a slow steady cadence and then rose slowly to a climatic shouting. Their bodies convulsed while these unintelligible words were being shouted. It was so moving that I began to be convinced that there was a demon inside of me. Ms. Brown was abundantly generous toward me with her time, prayers and love. Whether this exorcism was necessary or not, it demonstrated her concern for me. She continued to offer me a home and comfort for the next eight months while I slept on her sofa. During that time, I saved money and tried to get my life back together in order to create the means for my wife and son to ultimately come join me. In the meantime, they had moved back to Guyana to live with Natalya's family as life in England was not bearable. They now at least had a support system to help sustain them while I was not there. The school calendar dictated my ability to make the trip down to Guyana to visit. I missed so much of my son's earliest years as I could only arrange visits during spring, summer and winter breaks from school.

By February of 2006, I had finally saved enough money to move out from Ms. Brown's home and into my own apartment. One week after moving, my family's paperwork began to be processed. Now the reality of my wife, son and soon to be new daughter's ability to immigrate to the United States began to settle in. This was no longer just a hope or dream. It was going to happen. We would finally be able to all be together and live as one family. It would still be many months before they would all be able to come, so I knew I had to save as much money as possible in order to get them here and to make the necessary preparations for their arrival. This unfortunately meant I could not spend any money to go down to Guyana to visit during any of my breaks from school. I would not be able to be there to witness the birth of my daughter. Additionally, that Christmas, because I could not afford travel to Guyana and to send money home at the same time, I stayed in the United States. I spent Christmas morning that year, one of the most sacred days in a Guyanese family's life, sitting on a park bench crying my eyes out because I could not be with my family. That memory will haunt me forever. At this point, I had not seen my wife and family in seven months.

CHAPTER 17

THE AMERICAN DREAM

"You cannot give up on the American dream. We cannot
allow our fears and our disappointments to lead us into
silence and into inaction."

- Marco Rubio

I n the spring of the next year, my wife was given a date for
the exit interview from Guyana to be conducted at the U.S.
embassy. I flew home to Guyana to be there for the interview
and, if all went well, to accompany her and my son and infant
daughter back to the United States. We arrived at the American
embassy at 5 a.m. for the 10 a.m. scheduled appointment. A
long line and long wait was typical at the American embassy as
it always appears that most of Guyana is trying to migrate. In
fact, there are arguably more Guyanese who live outside their
homeland than inside. Despite the natural beauty, pristine
green lush of the rainforests and quaint houses of the
countryside, my homeland does not have the usual tourist
appeal of glamorous hotels along sandy beaches typically found
nearby throughout the Caribbean. To date, the unique local
customs, foods, fauna and animals have not been enough to
keep Guyanese at home or draw others to visit. The limited
economic opportunities encourage most Guyanese to seek a
more successful life elsewhere. My own parents were well aware

of this reality as they too sought a better life for themselves and for their children.

I was terrified the day of the interview as I felt my entire life was riding on its outcome. The entire process was nerve-racking. The officials at the United States embassy interviewed my wife first and then me. We had to show that our marriage was a genuine marriage as people often enter into arranged marriages for exorbitant amounts of money solely for the purpose of getting an exit visa to the United States. The cost of that arrangement can reach upwards of five times the average annual income of a Guyanese citizen. Although in recent years there has been a greater focus on uncovering these shams, immigration officials have historically sought to verify relationships before issuing visas. We therefore were required to produce documentation of communication between us in the years we were apart as well as photographs to show that we were in fact married. After what felt like an eternity, we were finally called by an immigration officer and told that the process was successful. The sheer joy I felt at that moment was indescribable. After five long years, a mortgaged future on a failed business, near death from malaria and typhoid, abuses inflicted by my distant cousin in England, and a Herculean effort to rebuild a life that had fallen apart, I would now finally be able to go home to the United States with my wife and family. God had provided for me again and I was now truly able to begin anew to seek the American dream. We obtained our visas the next day and left for the United States to pursue the life we dreamed about.

We landed at Miami International airport on March seventeenth, and after what seemed like an eternity, we cleared customs. I proudly walked my family out to my sixteen-year-old car and home to Coral Springs, Florida. We were starting from scratch, but at least we had our family intact. The first place my wife visited was the neighborhood supermarket. We bought groceries and set up house to begin our new lives in America. This was the most joy I had felt in a very long time as not only did I feel a sense of accomplishment in being able to bring my family to the country I loved, but I finally had achieved the goal I had been working towards: a family that could now all live and grow together. The value of all of the sacrifices I endured was now made clear. I believed God had now rewarded me for all of the hardships I had gone through.

Once my family had settled in to the routine of this new American life, we reflected on what we wanted to accomplish and how we could improve our lifestyle. We concluded that the only way we could advance ourselves economically was for my wife to go to school. I accompanied her when she went to take the entrance exam for the local college and after doing exceedingly well on the entrance exam, was accepted into the program to earn an Associate of Arts degree. Knowing that things would be difficult financially without Natalya's bringing in any income, I knew that the investment in her education was better for us in the long run. So, I took on a second job in order to sustain our family as she made her way through school.

Education is the key for any person willing to sacrifice for the American dream. However, advancement of one's position in life will not magically occur because you pursue additional education. Of course, the learning of new skills is what creates the foundation for advancement, but successful growth requires one more factor: determination. Whether it is the determination to learn the necessary aspects of a skill in school or for work, there is no task that is insurmountable when the determination is there. Nothing can prevent achievement of a goal except for a lack of effort. Despite the fact that I am presently approaching the end of my PhD program, I could not pass the relatively simple entrance exam for the high school I was supposed to attend in Guyana. In light of my present intellectual pursuits I can believe that I had the academic ability to pass that test, but what I was lacking was the determination. There were no educational opportunities in Guyana and no benefit to receive from them like there is in America. Additionally, I had no one encouraging me to pursue those academic achievements, so the drive was absent. Once I moved to the United States and saw how important an education was to success, I developed the determination to acquire whatever skills were necessary to succeed.

This lesson of education fueled by determination is one that I hold for myself, but I also continually teach it to my students. Even those who are academically gifted may seem to find mediocrity to be acceptable as they lack the drive to excel. There are no boundaries to one's achievements if one is brave enough to dream and pursue those dreams. When we limit ourselves to artificial barriers, the result is our acceptance of that limitation. More often than not, people will, for a variety of reasons, believe they are not capable of reaching a particular goal. I have seen it time and time again that when that barrier is lifted, and the individual gets the right incentive to reach a goal, then success ensues. For me, it has always been my faith in God and knowing of His love for me that has driven me to reach my goals. He has never let me down and has always guided me in my pursuits. Therefore, I know I cannot let Him down. I set my goals of which I believe He will approve and do what I must to succeed. One's beginning does not determine his end. No matter what one's age or circumstance, the combination of determination and education is unbeatable. With faith in one's own abilities coupled with the drive to hone one's skills, the American dream is always within reach.

With my belief in the power of education, through great sacrifice on my part, and no less dedication and commitment on my wife's part, I managed to not only earn my Master's degree, but also to help facilitate her being able to earn both an Associate and the Bachelor's degree. By saving every penny and my working two jobs, we were able to achieve the American dream of owning a beautiful home in one of the better neighborhoods of the county. My children were happy. They were safe, and we had accomplished in a few short years what many people struggle to achieve in a lifetime. God had blessed us abundantly. We continued to use the stimulus of education to strive for our greater potential as a professor from my master's degree program encouraged me to continue on with doctoral studies. Additionally, my wife set her sights on earning an MBA as she was not fulfilled in her employment as a teacher. I encouraged her to pursue her dreams as it was my belief that through continued studies we could better ourselves both individually and collectively as a family. Although Natalya would not be working while she pursued her MBA, the plan was for me to work double-time so she could reach her potential. In that way, as my working years began to taper, she would be in a better position to help carry the family later. We would pull each other up and rise as a family.

CHAPTER 18

THE HARDEST GOODBYE

"If I had a flower for every time I thought of you, I could
walk in my garden forever."

- Alfred Lord Tennyson

On one of the rare occasions when there was some free
time in her schedule, Natalya decided to search for
Father Tom. At this point I had not heard from him in well
over two years. I missed my friend dearly. One evening shortly
after her quest to find Father Tom began, I came home to
terrible news. In Natalya's search, she had discovered an
obituary for Father Tom. He had died a year earlier. The cancer
that had once ravaged his body had returned with a vengeance
and had taken his life. At the moment when I heard the news, I
wept uncontrollably for hours. This man was the only true
parent I had ever known. He had taken me off the street and
given me life. He taught me compassion, love of intellectual
pursuits, patience, diligence, hard work, sacrifice and kindness.
Everything I became was because of him. In my darkest hours I
could call him and after a few words of encouragement I would
be able to get back on track, overcoming whatever obstacle
blocked my path. Father Tom was my lifeline to existence. I felt
a sense of hopelessness and despair unlike anything I had ever
felt before. I had lost the only father I had ever known and was
not even there to witness his funeral or say goodbye.

When despair sinks in, the natural inclination is to begin to feel sorry for oneself. It is so much easier to wallow in one's sorrow than to find a way out of it. Through Father Tom's guidance, I have learned and used as a guiding principle to block that thought from emerging and taking hold. What good does it do to feel sorry for oneself for the things that go wrong in life? The longer one wallows, the further one falls back away from his original goal. It is inevitable that setbacks will occur in life, so to expend energy on nonproductive thoughts only saps the energy necessary to move forward in reaching a desired end. I have certainly endured setbacks, hardships and defeats— sometimes I believe more than my share—but it is imperative not to dwell in that self-pity place too long. Although sadness and anger may be the first emotional response, self-pity cannot take control. Any of these negative forces can put one in such a dark place from which one never gets out. If one stays in this void for too long, one may never find a way out, or, in the extreme, thoughts of suicide can begin to creep into the mind. In either case, one's ultimate potential is taken away.

Father Tom would forever remind me of this trap of self-pity. If I displayed any inkling of wallowing, in his sarcastic, endearing way, he would rub his thumb and index finger together next to his ear and tell me that he was playing the world's smallest violin while I was telling him my sad story. Through this sarcasm, I was taught to find my strength and to keep my thoughts away from self-pity. I learned that my resolve to get out of that dark place any time I faced a hardship stems from God and my faith in Him. I believe He has always protected me, so even after a defeat, I know I will land on my feet because of His love and care for me. I know I can always count on that faith as a starting point to find fortitude for the purpose of getting past the despair and moving forward. Everyone has a starting point to find his strength, so if it is not in God, look deep inside to find what it is that enables belief in oneself. The key is not to get stuck in the negativity and darkness. Instead, the focus should be on a way to move forward. Finding the energy and strength to propel progress will allow one to find a way out of the dark place, beyond the despair and ultimately back on the path to better days and into the light.

After hearing Father Tom's voice in my head and remembering his violin playing, I picked myself up in order to move forward. I was not going to allow a feeling of despair to control me. Father Tom taught me the skills I needed to both survive and thrive in life. I would rely on those skills many times over throughout my life, and at this most devastating point in time, I knew he would not want me to dwell in that dark place. I needed to move forward. The best way I could ever honor the greatest man I have ever known is to live the life he taught me to live.

The next winter break from school we decided to take a road trip to New Jersey with the primary purpose of visiting Father Tom's grave. After calling the former rectory where he worked, we were told where Father Tom was buried. On a cold winter's day shortly after Christmas, I walked into the Fairlawn cemetery and found his grave marker. Even though I knew he was dead, I still could not believe it was really him under the cold frozen earth. I knelt at his grave while my tears flooded my face and continued to fall to the frigid ground. My children stood in the distance and watched me cry. I have never been one to hide my emotions well, and this occasion was no different. I just wanted to cry for the deep loss I felt. There is no denying the love I felt. Stooping there, looking at his name etched into the stone marker, there was an undeniable reality inscribed in my heart. Here lay my real father. He taught me, guided me, provided for me, cared for me and, most of all, loved me. He was no longer with me physically, but I knew then and continue to know, that he will be with me spiritually until I take my last breath on this planet.

I have now committed myself to living the life for which Father Tom prepared me. I have accepted the fact that my parents never really wanted me as difficult as that is to conceive since I do not believe that one should bring children into this world and then abandon them. My own children were taken from me, but when they were with me, all I ever wanted was to take care of them and to teach and love them in the ways that Father Tom had taught and loved me. I created a stable home and nurturing environment and did everything within my power to give them every opportunity to be successful. All the things I did for my family were the things that were never done for me as I know how much I suffered because of that lack. My greatest hope was that I could offer my children everything I did not have when I was a child. I did not choose the life my children have now, and though my ex-wife has tried to sever the relationship I have with them, I pray every day that with God's help, my children will never doubt the love their father had and continues to have for them. The love that Father Tom showed me is the love I feel for my children. As an adult, I now embrace all the values that Father Tom taught me when I was a child. I believe that although evil exists, man is basically good. I realize that life is not always fair or kind, but with my faith I have learned how to get beyond that. I trust in a higher power and leave any injustices done against me to be handled by Him as I make my way through this odyssey called life. Monsignor Thomas Zazella, I have dedicated my master's degree, earned June 12, 2015, to you, the only father I have ever known.

CHAPTER 19

THE DREAM BECOMES A NIGHTMARE

"Every stumble is not a fall,
and every fall does not mean failure."

- *Oprah Winfrey*

Within just a few years of coming to the United States, with my help and assistance, Natalya earned two degrees. I worked two jobs, saved every penny, and ultimately purchased a beautiful home in a desirable section of town. This dream of home ownership certainly came true through hard work and much sacrifice, and having this dream become reality felt incredible. I was beyond excited when I signed the closing documents when we purchased the home. I believed that we all would have a permanent home and would no longer ever have to move from place to place.

To make this house feel more like a home, I spent hundreds of dollars and countless hours planting and caring for fruit trees in the backyard. These trees were to represent the permanency of our home as a family as well as my love for Natalya and the children. As they grew, they would become places for the children to climb and play. They also were to help Natalya feel closer to the home she missed in Guyana. Her childhood home was located in a region of Guyana known for bearing some of the best fruits the world over. By planting these trees in the backyard, she not only had the visual connection to her birthplace, but she had fruits to savor that memory as well. My heart and soul went into that home in order to make her happy and to give the children everything I did not have when I was a child.

Not too long afterwards, a perfect storm began to brew. The American dream which I had worked so hard to attain began to unravel. Natalya was in school full time pursuing her Master of Business Administration. I was accepted into and began a doctoral program, and our two salaries were not going far enough to sustain our expenses. We started to fall behind on the mortgage payments just as the bubble of the real estate market was about to burst. We continued to struggle to pay our monthly mortgage and maintain some semblance of normalcy in our family. The both of us struggling with academic requirements for graduate school, maintaining the household and children, and fighting off the potential foreclosure on our home, all were taking a serious toll on our family.

Money was so extremely tight that it created such desperate times for us. An evening out for us might include a trip to the mall just to people watch. That would be our entertainment. We might also purchase a large order of fast food French fries to share. We would savor every bite of those fries in order to make them last as long as possible since that was all the food we were going to have for that meal. This stress was compounded by my wife as she continued to send money to her family in Guyana—money that we desperately needed. There was no regard for our dire financial issues or my worries. Her main concern was her own family's plight while my main concern was Natalya's happiness. I was so deeply in love with her, I was never able to deny her when she asked for something. I therefore did not attempt to stop her from sending this money to Guyana. That decision only deepened the wound that was bleeding us dry as well as creating a larger rift between the two of us. Looking back, I realize what a disastrous mistake that was.

Over time we fell far behind on the house payments. Even though we had retained the services of a well-respected real estate attorney, our house ultimately went into foreclosure and our American dream went up in smoke. I was heartbroken once more when we lost the house. Upon being forced to give our home back to the bank, we suffered the humiliation of watching our neighbors see us pack our belongings and move to a rental townhouse. This brought back memories of when, after my parents divorced, my mother, sisters and I were continually forced to relocate to new rental homes. We would try to leave under the cover of twilight so as not to draw too much attention to ourselves when we were kicked out of one rental residence and needed to move to another. The embarrassment I felt as we walked along the public road carrying what few belongings we had will never be forgotten. Now, having the bank evict us out of our home put me right back into that mindset. This time, however, it was worse as I was passing that memory onto my own children. They too had to feel that same embarrassment that I felt as a child and there was no darkness in which to hide. They lost their home, their neighborhood and their comfort zone. There are few things more painful than watching your dreams slip away while there is not a single thing that can stop it from happening. The beautiful trees I had planted for my children to climb and to make my wife happy were now also gone. Our beautiful home and my long years of sacrifice were all for naught. I was heartbroken once more when we lost the house but knew that I needed to pick myself up, yet again, and move on for the sake of my family.

CHAPTER 20

ONE LAST TRY

"Failure at some point in your life is inevitable,
but giving up is unforgivable."

- Joe Biden

If I have learned anything at all in this lifetime, it is that nothing stays the same. After losing our home, we moved to a rental townhouse. Although the children adjusted relatively quickly and made new friends in the neighborhood, I took a little more time. My dream of home ownership was so important to me that losing our property weighed heavily on my heart. Eventually, however, I too adjusted as I have always done in the past. Being able to accept one's reality is paramount to survival, so adapting and being flexible is the key. In order to do that I turned my focus to the future and looked towards the advancement we would all enjoy once Natalya graduated with her MBA. This was all a part of the plan we had created. Now, after I had worked multiple jobs carrying Natalya through her undergraduate and graduate degrees, she would in turn help contribute to the family with her ability to obtain higher paying employment.

Graduation day took place about one year after moving into the townhouse. It truly ranks as one of the happiest days of my life. I was so proud of Natalya's accomplishment and was excited about all of the potential she could reach while the family would in turn benefit. On the day of the graduation, Natalya dressed in her finest outfit and I tried to make her feel as special as possible. My sister as well as Natalya's mother came in from out-of-state, and Natalya's sister and niece both flew in from South America all to celebrate the auspicious occasion. I made the day as significant as I possibly could and spared no expense to make it as enjoyable and memorable as possible for everyone but especially for my wife. After the graduation ceremony I treated everyone to dinner and drinks at one of the finest of restaurants. Everyone seemed happy as we celebrated Natalya's accomplishment and promise of a better future. It should have, however, been a red flag when she did not thank me among the people for whom she expressed gratitude for helping her achieve her accomplishment. Her bright future was not going to include me.

Now, armed with the power of a MBA, Natalya aspired for greener pastures in the hope of making a fresh start after the events of the past year. We decided that we would move to New York, the capital of the business world. The plan was that business opportunities would be more prevalent and available for her while I could find a better paying job as a teacher. We had saved enough cash to last us several months. So that we could save on expenses while looking for employment, we arranged to live with Natalya's family. By the time summer would be over we hoped to have new jobs, a new place to live and the children settled in a new neighborhood. So, on the day after graduation, all of the family that had come to celebrate Natalya's accomplishment helped us pack as we prepared for the move. Everything we owned went into a pack and ship container while the remainder of our belongings went in our truck and SUV. I had managed to save approximately thirteen thousand dollars to move us to New York and sustain us while we searched for employment and a place to live on our own.

Off we headed to New York to start what we believed would be a better life for us as a family.

The first indication that there would be trouble in New York was the fact that seven of us were now going to live in a one-bedroom apartment without air-conditioning in the middle of summer. Although we were grateful to have a place to live allowing us to save on expenses, our moving from a four-bedroom home in a gated community to a one-bedroom basement apartment, without air-conditioning, was quite an adjustment. If the temperature was ninety degrees outside, it was easily ninety-eight degrees inside. The sleeping arrangements were difficult as well. Natalya and I were stuck on an air mattress while my daughter and son were each relegated to their own uncomfortably small sofa. The landlord, who was my mother-in law's friend, took liberties with us as well, subjecting my children to disciplinary actions. She took control over the children and believed it to be her right to advise and control them, notwithstanding the fact that both their parents were living there and present as well. On one occasion, the landlady purposely locked my daughter out of the house because she did not approve of her clothing. Imagine the anger and frustration I felt watching a total stranger take control over my child and impose such a callous punishment while disregarding my parental authority. This new life in New York in no way resembled the life I had provided for my children in Florida. I was disgusted for allowing myself to be talked into this situation and continuing to allow it to happen. The landlady's treatment of my daughter made me realize we needed a change quickly. I can take any punishment a person or society inflicts on me, but not if it affects my children.

Coupling our far from ideal living situation and our limited financial resources, the motivation to find employment was extremely high. Natalya and I both began submitting resumes immediately upon our arrival to New York. Despite our efforts, we were not very successful in the interview process. Natalya did not even manage to procure a single interview the entire time we were there. The days of summer dragged on while we were spending over one-hundred thirty dollars a day. We were blowing through our resources and I knew something had to change.

After the bulk of the summer had passed and the prospects for employment, as well as our meager savings, were quickly disappearing, I became very stressed for my family. My hope to live in a nice neighborhood and regain the lifestyle I had worked for appeared to be evaporating as I was again being dragged back into the neighborhood and lifestyle I wanted to rise above. This time, however, I was going back down with my family. My children were experiencing a life I never wanted them to know. I had sacrificed so much in order to get them as far away from this kind of life. I did not see any promising resolutions to our predicament, so I urged my wife to consider moving back to Florida. I had taken a leave of absence from my employment thus ensuring that I would get my job back if I so desired. Regardless, she balked at the idea and remained adamant about being in New York with her family.

Because of the heat, when we slept in the basement we would leave a little side window open to allow air into the apartment. For purposes of having some ventilation, hot air is better than no air. This basement window looked out onto the street in front of the apartment on which there were plants that the landlady would water every morning. One morning, in what I believe was an act to "encourage" us to vacate the basement apartment, the landlady directly aimed the hose though the open window in order to empty the current of water inside our living quarters. The water sprayed my sleeping son from top to bottom soaking him completely. He jumped off the sofa dripping wet, and the splash from the water that drenched him soaked me as well. I was furious. I went upstairs to confront that heartless woman. She pled innocence saying it was an accident. At that point my mind was made up. This was the proverbial straw that broke the camel's back. I was moving back to Florida regardless of what my wife said or did as I was no longer going to subject my children to this inhumane treatment.

It is still hard to comprehend that persuading my wife to leave this unbearable living arrangement was so difficult. Whether she was already planning on her exit from the marriage or whether she just wanted to be with her mother, her insistence on staying in New York was perplexing. Nonetheless, after much continued pleading with her, she acquiesced. We once again loaded our trucks with our personal belongings and made our way back to Florida. We had no home to which to return and our savings had dwindled to almost nothing. After living in a hotel for a few days we managed to secure a nice three-bedroom apartment for our family. We unloaded our trucks, got settled, and the following day my wife and I flew back to New York to retrieve the rest of our belongings. We rented a truck, and I drove it back to Florida. So we began what I thought would be the second phase of our lives after learning a costly and painful lesson from our failed move to New York.

Chapter 21

Three Times Isn't a Charm

"It is easy to hate and it is difficult to love. This is how the whole scheme of things works. All good things are difficult to achieve; and bad things are very easy to get."

- Confucius

Upon our return to Florida, I went and spoke to my former principal and got my job back. My wife at this time had resigned her position and could not find employment. She decided she no longer wanted to teach elementary students and would not go back to her old job because of her strained relationship with the principal. She then decided she wanted to teach at the middle school level in my area of expertise, social studies. I provided her with all the materials I could find and tutored her in the subject matter until she was prepared to take the test. Soon afterwards, Natalya took the test and passed. She began applying for positions at different schools and shortly thereafter was hired at my old school.

Perhaps two weeks into Natalya's new position I started to detect a marked change in her behavior. She had never been one to talk a lot, but she was especially quiet for days on end. I tried to engage her in conversation to find out what was bothering her. She still would not say. I continued to press the issue until she finally opened up and told me the truth: she was unhappy in our marriage. I was devastated. I had tried to give her everything she ever wanted, including a lifestyle, the likes of which she never would have enjoyed in Guyana. She said she would be my friend, and she would come and cook for me, but she did not want to be in the marriage any more. I could not believe what I was hearing, especially in light of all the sacrifices I felt I had made on behalf of my family. Her devastating words went even so far as to describe how she envisioned a new life for herself, including how she would be intimately involved with another man. This woman, the one that I loved with all my heart, for whom I endured countless sacrifices, and for whom I had given up everything, cold-heartedly was able to describe to me how she would be intimate with someone else. The avalanche overtaking me continued even as she suggested that this was not my fault. Perhaps, she said, I was too good for her. Of course, I now realize her intent was to soften the initial blow as those words would take an about face once the court system got involved. I begged and pleaded with her not to go, but at this point she had made up her mind to leave.

I could not see the point of continuing my life without my wife. Everything I had built, everything I had worked for, and everything I had sacrificed for was now going to walk out the door and take my children in tow. With the mindset that nothing in my life mattered except for my family, I went to my gun closet, retrieved my handgun, cocked it, and put it to my head. Natalya came over and started to beg me to put it down. She promised she would stay if I would just put the gun down. I believed her; I suppose I believed her because I needed to believe her, and so I put the gun down.

Things calmed down around the house for a few days, but eventually my wife made it clear she wanted to leave. Devastated, I tried once more to take my life. This time it was with a knife, and this time again she stopped me. At the time, not only could I not see that I was delaying the inevitable, but I could not see the devastating effects I was inflicting, and would have inflicted, on my family. My myopic focus was all about not losing the family unit. Despite my overarching intent to keep my family together, my wife wanted to be free regardless of the consequences to me or the children. To this day, I still do not fully understand her motivations to sever our family. Nonetheless, it is done and there is no return or repair.

As time went on and the holidays were approaching, my sister Joan had invited us to Illinois to spend Thanksgiving with her. We had all been looking forward to the road trip and the children were excited. I could sense that my wife's heart was not in it, but at the last minute she decided to go. I saw this as an opportunity for us to try to work things out and somehow repair the marriage. The trip to Illinois was seventeen excruciatingly quiet hours. The only time my wife would speak to me was to give directions or to ask for a bathroom or food break for the children. Yet, I was hopeful. I knew she was very close with my sister Joan and perhaps there was some way my sister could speak to her and encourage her to try to work things out in the marriage.

After speaking to Natalya, Joan recommended that I get on my knees and apologize. I did as she suggested with tears streaming down my face, but to no avail. I had found myself in this position on a number of previous occasions as well. One time in particular, Natalya actually laughed at me and accused me of being "a weak and pathetic man." I am not sure why I thought this time around I would receive a more promising result, but I was so determined to keep my family together in any way possible, that I would have done anything. My world was ripping apart at the seams and my children had front row seats for this nightmare. The drive back from Illinois to Florida was even more painful as we talked even less than on the ride north. I had asked my wife to let me stay in Illinois if she knew she would be leaving me when we came back to Florida. The fact that she asked me to come back to Florida with her allowed me to falsely assume that she would give the marriage a try. I was wrong again.

The final event that precipitated the end of my marriage to the point of no-return was my third suicide attempt. My wife made it abundantly clear that she was going to leave at an opportune moment, but I was not told when that moment would be. All I knew was that I was going to lose the family for which I had sacrificed beyond belief and my sole purpose for living was about to go up in flames. I was certain that I did not want to be a party to that end. I therefore made up my mind that this time around, I was going to be successful at ending my life as for all intents and purposes it seemed to be over already.

While the children were in their room playing video games, and my wife was in the kitchen angry and ignoring me as usual, I went into our bedroom and locked the door. I had showered earlier, and the floor of the shower was still a bit slippery. At this point, I shut down all logical thought and was focused exclusively on one end. I looked around the bedroom, saw a computer cord, and decided on my choice of method. With warm tears running down my face, I wrapped one end of the cord around my neck and walked to the shower door beam overhanging the shower and wrapped the other end around it. Without another thought, I closed my eyes and allowed myself to slip and fall on the slick, soapy floor. As far as I knew it was done.

The last thing I remember was allowing myself to fall. I fell into the most peaceful sleep I had ever imagined possible. I was walking down a road, a country road, one unfamiliar to me. It was not a bright sunny day, but it was certainly a gorgeous day. I remember there being trees sparsely scattered on both sides of the road. I know I was not walking away from anything on that road. I was walking slowly with a purpose toward something. There was a door, a simple door, in the middle of the roadway. I never got there because I felt a hard hit on my shoulder and my beautiful dream was over. I was conscious once more and my wife and kids were crying as I lay flat on the bathroom floor.

Based on my wife's account of the three minutes during which I was apparently unconscious, she said she heard me call for her. To this day I cannot remember calling for her, but she said she heard it distinctly. Upon hearing my call, she went to the door and realized that I had locked the door and there was no way of her getting the door open. She started to panic outside the door struggling to get into the bedroom. Somehow, she managed to pick the lock and started to call for me when she could not see me in the room as I had pushed the bathroom door closed behind me. When she looked in the bathroom she recalled seeing me hanging there with my face ashen white and my tongue hanging out of my mouth. She said she immediately tried to get the cord from around my neck, but because of my bodyweight, she could not release it. She then tried to get my eleven-year-old, sixty-five pound son to help her lift my body to get the cord from around my neck. Even with his help, they could not loosen the cord as I was just too heavy for the both of them to lift. At that point she instructed my eight-year-old daughter to join in the effort to try to help lift me, but again to no avail. I was too heavy and as the minutes passed away, I crept closer to death. The next thing Natalya attempted to do was have my son climb to the top of the shower rod while she and and my daughter tried to lift me so that my son could loosen the cord from around my neck. They ultimately were successful in that final attempt. As I fell to the floor, my wife told me she first tried hitting my face to bring me back and when that did not work, she then proceeded to slap me even harder on my shoulders multiple times to bring me back. At some point in whatever state I was in, I felt the slap on my shoulder and regained consciousness. That period of three minutes as my wife and the children struggled to get the cord from around my neck, I was dying or even possibly dead. At the very least, I was unconscious based on my memory loss and my wife's account of the incident.

That experience has changed me profoundly as I whole-heartedly believe that it was divine intervention that saved me that night. No other explanation makes any sense as my death would have made my wife's life so much easier for her. She would not have had to go through the stress of going out on her own and being a single mother, and she would have been able to reap the benefits of being my beneficiary. I believe it was God working through Natalya who was underpinning her gallant efforts in saving me. I believe He spared me that night as I have not yet completed my designated task here on earth. The belief that when it is one's time to go must also hold the opposite as true: when it is not one's time to go, life will continue. Apparently, it is not yet my time to go, so I must still have a purpose to fulfill here on earth. Perhaps some of my intended purpose includes my being able to share this experience with others. I realize now that trying to commit suicide was wrong and flies in the face of my cherished relationship with God, my ultimate love. By sharing my experience with others who may be contemplating a similar course of action, perhaps because of my firsthand experience I will have enough credibility to convince them to choose otherwise. My choice was one of desperation and lack of thought. Hopefully, I can inspire others to feel and think beyond their despair.

Natalya was now more than ever determined to leave. Her exit finally came several days later when I tried to convince her to change her mindset. I invited my friend Bernard over to act as an intermediary in the hopes that he would help provide a civil and logical perspective. What happened instead was Natalya tried to persuade Bernard to see her viewpoint. While we were sitting on the patio, she made him all kinds of food and beverages and then, to get him on her side, told him I had accused her of sleeping with him. Bernard and I had a friendship of almost three decades which she then proceeded to destroy. A fleeting thought which I shared with my wife in an ancient intimate moment was now being used to destroy my friendship with my best friend. It was evident that she hated me and wanted out of our relationship at any cost. After putting that accusation out in the open, she then proceeded to curse me like she had never cursed before. She dug into me with a profanity laced tirade the likes of which I had never heard before, except perhaps from my father. Bernard at that point suggested that he and I leave to go get something to eat. In retrospect, that was the opportunity Natalya was waiting for. As I was trying to force down a cup of soup at the restaurant, Bernard's phone rang. He passed it to me. I will never forget the words my wife said to me that night. It would be the last words that would be exchanged between us. Actually, it would be the last words that I would hear from her because what came next left me speechless. She said to me, "I have left and taken the kids, you can go ahead and kill yourself now." This is the woman that I had given everything to, including my life, saying these words to me. I immediately gave my friend the phone and started to run the two miles to get home. While I ran, I prayed and hoped against all odds that I heard wrong. No such luck. I walked into an empty apartment. She was gone and had taken the children.

Chapter 22

The Plummet

"Tragedy is a tool for the living to gain wisdom,
not a guide by which to live."

- Robert Kennedy

My life after that moment went into free fall. I did not know which direction to take. I had no anchor, no rudder and no idea what I was supposed to do. My whole purpose in life was now gone. I tried to find out from anyone I could whether Natalya was planning on coming back. She told people that it was just a temporary split and would come back in a couple of days because she believed me to be mentally unstable. Time has proven that she never intended to come back to me. Rather, she had gotten all she could from me, at least so she thought, and was now going to strike out on her own. I suspect that I was a pawn in her fourteen year plan to escape a third world life and attain the American dream. Natalya used all of the training and refining I could offer to get her to a point of individual strength. Now, she would reach higher without me. In order to achieve that goal, she would need to amass ammunition to cultivate the backing of our friends and family. Using my weaknesses and the advantages of the American legal system, she could support her actions notwithstanding her motivation. The picture she painted of me to justify her move equated me with the devil himself.

I knew I had to hang on to my job because it was all I had left. As hard as it was to get up every morning, I knew I had to show up. Some days I could barely make it ten minutes without knowing whether or not I was going to make it another ten minutes. I leaned on anyone who would lend me an ear or a shoulder just to get through this devastation. My life at school during this time was a nightmare. My wife had told someone at her school that I had attempted suicide which eventually caused rumors to spread through my school. Word got back to my principal, who promptly called me down to her office to make sure I was alright. I appreciated her concern but felt terribly embarrassed knowing everyone knew my personal issues and what I had done. Getting through those days took every ounce of energy I could muster. I was blessed to have a few very supportive friends who held my hand every step of the way until I was able to stand on my own two feet again. I frequently found the need to take time away from my class to escape to the bathroom and cry when the emotions overcame me. I even reached out to my biological father for comfort. If I could have crawled under the earth and gotten to Father Tom's comforting hands, that is what I would have done. I had never felt such intense hurt and loss.

I managed to hang on and get to Christmas break. My sister Joan came down from Illinois to try and comfort me, but no earthly being can comfort a broken and shattered man. As much as my family and close-knit circle of friends tried, my day to day existence was the greatest challenge I had ever faced. It would be lying to say that I did not entertain thoughts again of leaving this world. My mind was completely broken. There was a point where I actually did not sleep for three nights straight. Not only could I not sleep, but I could not eat or even think logically. My life was spinning out of control. I was in such a dark place that I knew I could not continue my doctoral studies, so I took one semester off from the program. Next to losing my family, leaving the program was a terrible blow. Just getting into the program had been a dream of mine, let alone attaining the PhD degree. I was terrified that I would not ever be able to pick myself up and get going again in my studies. As much as the thought of leaving the program terrified me, I was too paralyzed by fear, depression and apprehension to continue my studies.

Although I doubted myself after the suicide attempt and questioned my life, my choices and my abilities, I never did give up on my faith. It sustained me through those trying times as it always has. God never fails man; man fails God as we are imperfect beings. I spent hours reading anything and everything I could to help me navigate this calamity in which I found myself. I read the Bible: Old Testament, New Testament, Psalms, prayers and any other biblical writings I could find. Although I have always had a strong belief in God, I now delved deeper into who my God is and what my relationship with Him is all about. As my faith was revitalized and my relationship with God was reaffirmed, my personal and physical strength was resurrected. It is this strength that would catapult me to a new level of existence, one which has helped enable me to overcome the continued obstacles I have faced and will continue to face.

I have come to rediscover the understanding that if one is to have true faith in a higher power, then one must accept all of His actions. When one is blessed, it is very easy to feel the love for God and thank Him for those gifts. A true test of faith, however, comes when the hardships prevail. If the belief, love and trust in God is truly present, then one must carry that belief, love and trust in Him not only during the high times of life but also during the low periods of life, most especially during those low times. No one can understand the mind of God, so it is futile to try to understand the reasons behind many life events. The best that can be done is to accept one's reality knowing that God, as creator of everything, is the only one with the full picture of life. He knows the end game for everyone, so our individual life events are just pieces of the full puzzle picture. Having faith in God means to believe in the positive consequences for each of those events as they move us further along to reach the destiny set out for us. Therefore, even events which can be perceived as devastating can turn into a gift as it propels one to a place where God intends us to be. Since the loss of my family, I have acknowledged that this storm I am weathering has enabled me to attain the closest relationship I have ever had to God. Feeling His love and having trust in Him is the greatest gift I could receive, and I would not have received it but for the breakup of my family.

Holding on to this deepened faith and rediscovered perspective, I knew that I needed to bring some sense of normalcy back into my life. Pulling from my strength in this faith as well as from the strength of my friends around me, I began to inch out of the black hole which had overtaken me. I thought about what was still within my power. I could not control Natalya's leaving or her spreading of untrue information about me, but I could control the direction of my own life. I could not put my family back together, but the next most important thing in my life was my education. I decided to get myself back into the doctoral program. I clawed my way over to the phone and made the call to the chairman of my program asking for permission to continue. He assented, so I enrolled in one course to see if I could handle the work. Having the academic focus back in my life provided a distraction from the pain of loss and helped restore my need for purpose. I put my whole self into my work which ultimately resulted in maintaining my perfect grade point average and getting me back on track.

CHAPTER 23

LOOKING FOR EQUILIBRIUM

"Yesterday is not ours to recover,
but tomorrow is ours to win or lose."

- Lyndon B. Johnson

T he next several months felt like purgatory for me. My day to day was brutal, but I knew the situation was temporary. I was praying for something to change for the better. Natalya and I lived apart and divided time with the children. I know how important being a full-time father is and the impact of not having one is detrimental to any child's development. I know this from firsthand experience. This division of time was not going to be sustainable as I needed my children to know I was there for them at all times. Nonetheless, for the interim, I spent every other weekend and one weeknight with them. The transition to single parenthood was difficult to say the least but being with my children was everything to me and so, I rose to the challenge.

Over the next few months I struggled to maintain an equilibrium in my daily life. Work and school were the primary focus. I went to work all day, gym in the afternoon and school work in the evenings and weekends. It was not an exciting life, but it helped me establish a routine that I could control. I began to learn to take care of my daily needs as well. Something as simple as making three meals each day became overwhelming.

I needed to start planning ahead to shop, to cook and to clean. For many days I was treading water, just getting by. On a rare occasion I could feel as if I took a step forward, but on other days, I lost footing. This back and forth continued for many months to the point where I remember thinking I was simply existing and that I would never be truly happy again.

A particularly difficult time was the day my daughter had a breakdown at school. She blurted out that her father had tried to kill himself which resulted in the Department of Children and Families becoming involved. DCF now required me to have supervised visits to be with my own children. Even though there was never any evidence of my being a threat to my children, I was now being told when I could be with them and judged as to how I would be with them. Every time I would try to bring some semblance of normalcy back to the house, DCF would show up at my door with police officers to check on me and the state of the children. They even followed me to the grocery store one day and showed up on my birthday as I was about to share some birthday cake with my children. In my entire life, I had never been involved with the law. Now, DCF and law enforcement were showing up almost once a week to my home. The word around my neighborhood was that I was crazy since I tried to commit suicide and whenever my children came to visit with me, my children's friends would tease them relentlessly. Natalya would later use this incident to procure the upper hand in gaining full custody of our children, notwithstanding the fact that there were never any findings that I was an unfit parent. My children were either being bounced back and forth from parent to parent or being ridiculed for events beyond their control. Enduring the collapse of my family was hard but watching the toll it was taking on my children was unbearable.

I suppose Natalya too did not see this shared arrangement as sustainable as she wanted full control over the children.

She prohibited their communication with me when we were not together and began to put stipulations on my ability to be with them. Ultimately, she exploited my actions, used my weaknesses and utilized the power of the legal system to manipulate custody issues so that I will not be the present father I have always wanted to be. Since the first couple of months of the separation, I have not had any contact or knowledge of the whereabouts of my children. That has been the hardest part of this storm to weather.

Divorce was the last thing I wanted as everything I had worked for was about creating and maintaining a family, but my wife dragged me to court kicking and screaming. Despite a lack of evidence, she put a temporary restraining order on me and soon after served me divorce papers. I refused to accept them at first but when the server decided to hang them on my door in full view of my neighbors, I finally relented.

I was advised to get a divorce attorney immediately. I did not have a hundred dollars to my name because my wife left me with several months of unpaid car payments and rent on a three-bedroom apartment to carry on my own. My sister, however, lent me two-thousand dollars to help me defend myself. I was in all kinds of trouble with no place else to go financially. I turned to everyone I knew to help me raise money to defend myself against my wife and her lawyers. It is still a mystery as to where she was getting the money to fight this fight.

CHAPTER 24

TIMING IS EVERYTHING

"Right actions in the future are the best apologies for bad
actions in the past."

- Tryon Edwards

It took me about four sittings to finally get through watching
the movie "Spotlight," which is the story of how the
investigative reporters from the *Boston Globe* uncovered the
decades-old Church sex abuse and coverup scandal. I had
buried those memories so deeply, I thought I would never recall
them. I intended to believe that they never happened.
Watching that movie was so difficult, I now realize that one can
never escape from or erase the past. It hit so close to home that
what was inappropriate for the producers to put on camera, I
was able to fill in the gaps quite vividly from my own
experiences.

The descriptions of the abuse were identical to my experiences. Most of the priests used charm to get to their prey.
Father Jose was different in his approach as he used his power
over me to do what he did. He took what he wanted because I
was in a dire position of need. Father Bradley, on the other
hand, perhaps because he did not have Father Jose's power,
used attention to get to his goal. As I watched the movie, the
more I began to tremble and become nauseated as I was forced
to relive those experiences all over again. I remembered walking

into Father Jose's private quarters sick as a dog, trusting and believing that he was going to help me get better. I needed to stop the movie several times so that it took me four different attempts to view the entire film. I felt the pain of each molested victim as the script proceeded. All the memories were brought back to light as though they never left. Now that the memories have been revived and I have begun to work through them, I now can say that I am eternally grateful for the reporters that broke this story. I can only hope that they know how much good they have done for the victims by exposing those morally bankrupt priests. I certainly was able to find comfort in knowing that I was not the only person who suffered that dehumanizing experience. I have learned that there are countless of us victims that struggle to deal with those past events.

Although "Spotlight" focused exclusively on the incidents in the Boston area, it is well-known that these heinous acts have occurred in dioceses all over the world. There are literally thousands of priests who have been accused of tens of thousands of sex crimes within the Catholic Church, which has paid out literally billions of dollars in settlement money for restitution. These claims date back to the earlier part of the twentieth century and continue through today. For almost one hundred years, there is documentation that priests have violated their religious, moral and legal responsibilities by taking advantage of other men, women and especially children. It has become clear through revealed documentation that not only have these incidents occurred, but the Church had knowledge of them and covered up the abuses by protecting the perpetrators, ignoring the victims and shielding the public.

Once the door of memory of this abuse was forced opened, I have had to confront the demons that surfaced from within. In my culture, there is nothing more shameful than to be a man who is raped by another man. I hid that experience for decades so as not to appear as less than a man in anyone's eyes. I never cared much about what my father thought of me, but in some way, I wanted to spare him the shame as well. Now, not only does my father have to deal with this realization, but my children will as well. I can only hope that they can understand that being raped and abused as a child was not something I willingly chose. It was cast upon me and has become one of the many burdens I have been destined to bear. I have learned that I am no less a man because of those experiences, rather I believe I have endeavored to be more of a man in spite of that experience.

Facing these demons has been an ongoing struggle and one which I believe will last a lifetime. Every victim labors to deal with them and every victim handles their individual struggle in a personal way. Counseling works for some while others resort to more severe measures such as drugs or even suicide. It is not uncommon for most victims to have unsettled lives at best or at the worst, lives cut short. Even one of the most well-known and outspoken advocates for victims of pedophiliac priests, James Thomas Kelley, wound up stepping in front of a commuter train in New Jersey to end his own life. Although the reasons for his suicide were not confirmed, it is surmised that his own demons were too overwhelming and ultimately overcame him. These unfathomable sex crimes committed by individuals who were supposed to be trusted, upright, God-fearing men truly unravel the necessary threads of social stability needed to navigate our world. I often wonder if my own experiences have stripped me of the ability to trust and to maintain meaningful relationships.

Thoughts of suicide have unquestionably entered my mind as I have admittedly attempted it several times. I believe those periods of despondency were inextricably linked to my experiences with Fathers Jose and Bradley. As much as I tried to bury those memories, I now understand there is no escaping them. Although I am keenly aware of the constant shadow of death surrounding my life, I recognize it and realize that it is a threat to my life. I combat those feelings with daily prayer and through strengthening my relationship with God. I refuse to believe that God has protected and provided for me my entire life to sit back and watch me end my own life. I have no doubt in my mind that God has sustained me as He has a purpose for me. As long as I do not waver from my trust and belief in Him and that belief of purpose, I will be able to put one foot in front of the other and move forward. I have concluded and gladly accepted that my purpose is here to help others who are suffering in any way so that there is a positive value to my experiences. I can only hope that all the other victims who struggle with those same demons can believe in their own purpose in life in order to repel their despondent thoughts and be able to live a more peaceful life.

Although some might call it a coincidence, I would say that it was divine intervention which offered me at last financial relief from my experiences with Fathers Jose and Bradley. One day during my planning period at work, I happened to read an article about how the Catholic Church was being exposed for pedophilia committed by priests. It continued that some of the victims had sued the Church and won. More significantly, I noticed some of these cases were from Paterson, just where I had spent some of my earlier years. I continued to follow the links of the story and sure enough, Monsignor Jose Alonso was a priest in the Archdiocese who was convicted of molesting some young men about the same time that ugly incident had happened to me at Saint John's. I read and believed I actually knew some of those young men, but this had been over thirty-five years prior. I saw how these victims had sued and won a settlement against the Church which gave me the hope that I could pursue this avenue as well. It could potentially become a means to provide emotional healing and some semblance of closure for that experience, for the Church to make amends, and additionally as a way to acquire financial help for the pending divorce proceedings which hovered over me. My back was up against the wall as I needed to defend myself against Natalya's allegations. The cost of retaining an attorney was significantly more than what I could afford, so I was in trouble once more. As always, however, God opened a door to provide me with a way out of my trouble. I did not know how to go about pursuing this course of action or even if there was a statute of limitations which would preclude me from getting any restitution. Nevertheless, I endeavored to try.

I spent some time online and researched the cases of the victims of these crimes. There seemed to be a common thread within many of these cases, which mirrored my own. Often, these boys were immigrant children, being raised by the Church without their own families. They felt beholden to their caregivers, so when a priest crossed a line and committed one of these heinous acts, they all too often were too afraid of being sent back to their home country from which they escaped or afraid of being reprimanded and, like me, put out on the street. It was overwhelming to me to see just how many cases there actually were. Without too much difficulty I was able to track down the attorney who had represented these young men. His name was Greg Gianfarcalo. I reached out to him for help.

Greg asked me to share my story with him. He verified my identity and called me back a few days later for an even more detailed version of the story. Needing to do his due diligence, he asked me for documentation, so he could continue his research into my claim. I gave him everything to which I had access and was able to provide very specific details which substantiated my claim. Notwithstanding the fact that these events occurred over thirty-five years earlier and I had buried them in the abyss of my mind, for a victim of abuse the events are forever etched in memory and readily recalled with the proper stimulus. After conducting this initial investigation, he accepted the case. Having my experiences confirmed not only let me pursue this course of action but also helped convince certain family members who up to this point had never believed in the validity of my abuse allegation. Two of my own sisters never believed me when I told them years ago what had happened. One sister in fact even laughed when I told her about it. My mother still refuses to accept the reality of what I experienced. I am not sure if it is because she chooses not to or that she is unable to accept it. My father, on the other hand, accepts the reality but has offered zero support or compassion for the anguish I endured. Perhaps he realizes that I never would have had to be in the care of the Church if he had never created an environment in his home from which I felt the need to leave.

I suppose the stigma attached to sexual molestation makes it difficult for people to know how to respond. As the victims themselves all have different ways of responding and coping, I suppose those differences also extend to the family and friends of the victims. My strategy was just to bury the events and try to carry on with life. I did not want to admit to the humiliation I felt or the shame I knew that others would potentially feel towards me. I had the love of Father Tom along with my deep rooted faith. I felt no need to revisit the events of the past as Father Tom was helping to prepare me for a future. My faith allowed me to see that God created within me the tools necessary for my survival, so I could continually utilize them in order to carry on in life. Now that I have been directed to uncover these past memories and have been able to bring the experience to light, I have been able to work past the shame and discomfort. I still strive to do God's will, so it is my greatest hope that only good can come out of those dreadful past events. It is my intention to use the lessons of those experiences in order to make a positive difference in the lives of others. My life will not be defined by the sad episodes of years gone by. My works moving forward will determine my epitaph.

Greg contacted the Catholic archdiocese and relayed to them my experiences with Fathers Jose and Bradley. It is amazing how the Catholic Church has put in place such a highly organized and efficient system to deal with these molestation claims. I suppose it has become necessary in light of the exorbitant number of cases with which they have been required to deal. After checking and rechecking my story, their representatives still required one more piece of evidence before it would accept any responsibility. They wanted to make sure that I was underage when all the events took place. In order to appease this request, Greg wanted to speak to my sister, so she could corroborate the timeline I had given him. After realizing that Marcy had moved out of the house and enlisted in the Air Force during much of the time that I lived with my father, Greg felt he needed to contact my father to corroborate the timeline of when I had actually left his home. Considering the treatment that I received from my father when I lived in his house, I was not sure whether he would even engage in a conversation. Greg insisted that he needed to try as that verification was essential to procure the Church's acceptance of liability which, in turn, would produce a settlement. Contact was in fact made by Greg, but my father conveniently could not recall the timing. He reported that all he could remember was that when he learned of the rape he referred to me as an "anti-man," the derogatory Guyanese term for homosexual. I was not surprised when I heard about the conversation because using that term allowed my father to shift responsibility away from him onto me, notwithstanding the fact that those encounters were forced upon me. He also was able to deflect responsibility by not confirming the timing since if he made the connection between his verbal and physical abuse to me and my need to leave his home then the consequences I endured would rest on his shoulders. He never took responsibility back then, so why would he do so now? An alternative source was now necessary for corroboration, so Greg asked if he could contact Maureen. I gladly gave him her number and will forever consider her my guardian angel. After speaking to Maureen, who of course verified all of the events I had relayed to him, Greg had all the evidence he needed to confront the Catholic Church.

Things moved quickly after accumulating the necessary information and verification. It was becoming clear that there would ultimately be a settlement with the Catholic Church. I could detect the excitement in Greg's voice as well. I came to learn that these cases, of which Greg handled hundreds, had personal meaning to him as many of his childhood friends were victims of the first priest to be defrocked by this scandal, the infamous James Hanley, who was laicized by the Church in 2003. Greg was consequently extremely passionate about helping the victims as well as making the Church accept responsibility for these actions. In order for the Archdiocese to ultimately settle with me, it required one last piece of evidence: a picture from my yearbook from the class of 1983 Paterson Catholic High School. This was a bit of a challenge as the school had since closed, but I could describe myself down to the clothes I wore that day. All these years later I can still remember what I wore because in order to take pictures for the yearbook, all male students were required to wear a jacket. I could not afford one, so I had to borrow one from a fellow student. Being embarrassed that I did not have the necessary clothes to wear, I will always remember the grey blazer I wore that day for pictures. After I would guess not too much of a search, the Archdiocese managed to acquire a yearbook along with a picture of Robert G. Lawrie, labeled "Most Congenial," wearing the grey blazer I had described.

Greg called me shortly after the picture was discovered in the yearbook and told me that the Archdiocese had agreed to settle. I was beyond thrilled on several accounts. Deciding to walk down this path and revisiting those memories truly was a godsend on many levels. Not only was the offense I suffered now going to be redressed, but I was provided a way to defend myself in the pending divorce case. I no longer had to keep begging everyone for money for my legal fees. Shortly after my case was verified by the Archdiocese, I received my settlement and immediately retained an attorney and began the ugly process of defending myself in the divorce action.

CHAPTER 25

FINDING A NEW PATH

"Hope deferred makes the heart sick,
but a longing fulfilled is a tree of life."

- Proverbs 13:12

Just like Job, who I have come to empathize with more and more, I have felt as if I had lost everything that mattered. My home, my friends, and above all, my family are now gone. After boundless sacrifices, my wife and children, my whole reason for being, are no longer a part of my reality. Moving into a one bedroom apartment, I have now been forced to recreate a new life for myself. More importantly, I have been forced to discover a new purpose for my life. Admittedly, this realization to discover a new purpose was not easy. I spent many months questioning my ability to handle a new reality and questioning why God would redirect me away from a path to which I was so committed. It was my countless readings of the Job story which ultimately led me to the rediscovery of God's blessings and love for me and the acceptance of an ultimate purpose for each of us. My challenge was to redirect my focus in order to discover my own new purpose. The proverbial lightbulb finally went on when I realized that in spite of all my disappointments and struggles, I was still being sustained and protected. There have certainly been numerous times when by all accounts I should not have survived, but for the grace of God I am still here. Therefore, I should be spending the rest of my days showing my gratitude for that protection and love. My new purpose became quite clear to me. The best way to show my gratitude and thankfulness is to do what God expects of us all: to show kindness and mercy to all of mankind. As it is written, "And what does the Lord require of you? To act justly, to love mercy, and to walk humbly with your God." Micah 6:8

I began to walk down this new path using my settlement money as a natural beginning to a new future. I used a portion of the money to create closure from my past. The first thing I did was to buy a plane ticket so that I could visit Maureen. I had not seen her in almost thirty years, yet when we reunited it was if I had never left. My love for her and her children had only grown stronger in the time I was away. Maureen's children were no longer children as time had them grow into adulthood. They all treated me as one of the family when I visited, and it truly felt like I had come home. I cannot even begin to describe the feeling I had knowing that I was now in a position to show her that I had worth and to thank her for believing in me and giving me the love of family,which gave me the opportunity to grow and develop roots.

After visiting with Maureen and her family in Massachusetts, I drove down to New Jersey to make peace with my biological father. I felt a strong need to see him. Notwithstanding all the ugliness I had heard he said about me concerning the abuse I suffered at the hands of the priests, I knew I needed to close that door behind me if I wanted to pursue a life of peace. I wanted him to know how I rose above the inequities I had endured and that in spite of his being such a negative force in my life, I have still been blessed.

Going to that house after so many years reawakened the nightmares that took place there. No matter how old I get, I suppose I will never be comfortable going to that house as it represents the intense trauma I endured as a child. Knowing that I was approaching the address created a terrible queasiness in my stomach. I walked up to the door that I was all too familiar with from so many years earlier. The memory of that long walk I took up those very stairs when my father picked me up at Paterson Catholic and had me walk those steps to put a beating on me so many years before came to mind so vividly. These were the very stairs that I had seen my stepmother leap over as she made her escape from the beatings my father inflicted on her. My knees were weak walking up those stairs then as all those memories came flooding back to me as I rang the doorbell. I knew there was nothing my father could do to me now, so I stood at the door and waited as I rang the bell. The nervousness was still there, and I pondered what I was really going to say to him. Do I try to get him to see the error of his ways? Do I forgive him? I will never know what words would ultimately have been uttered as the door never opened. Instead of a conversation, I left my father a gift: a book of prayers. I hope he reads it, finds inspiration from within it, and lives the rest of however many years he has left in a way in which God would approve. I know it will not change my past or our relationship, but hopefully, it will help him in his preparation for his next life. I won't see him again in this life unless he chooses to see me graduate from my PhD program. That will be his choice.

After my visit with my biological father, I went to visit the only father I had ever known, Father Tom. He lay in his grave and I had a strange sense of peace as I stared at the grave marker. I do not know how long I stood there, but I felt Father Tom's spirit within me. I may not have been there when he died, but for the rest of my living years, he is a part of my being as the air I breathe. My visit this time was during the summer and the area around his grave was nice, green, and clean. This was a sharp contrast to the first time I had seen his grave which was in the winter. At that time, it was cold and gray outside and the ground in which he lay was frozen solid. As I stood there connecting spiritually, this change of season did not go unnoticed. There was a rebirth not only in the cemetery grounds, but in my own spiritual outlook as well. I stood at his grave for quite a while and focused on the impact this one man had on my life. He has been gone from this world for almost a decade, yet his words and deeds continue to inspire, motivate and propel me forward to make a difference in this world. I believe he is watching over me and guiding me. It became so clear to me that all along Father Tom's guidance was meant to put me on this path of living a life of acting justly, loving mercy, and walking humbly with God.

All of the pieces of my life now clearly seem to fit in the overall picture of this path. My career as an educator has always allowed me to impact the lives and minds of many. I have had the opportunity to encourage countless students to reach for heights they never thought possible as well as to provide emotional and financial support for many who lack those resources. Coming from an immigrant, abusive household, I have experienced the feelings of not fitting in, not being the same as everyone else, not having what everyone else has, not feeling confident about my abilities, and not feeling loved. Although I have always had the opportunities to aid those students with similar experiences, now that focus has become paramount.

As I prepare my dissertation proposal in the area of research methodology, I now know with certainty that the first study I will undertake as a PhD researcher will be suicide in Guyana. Sadly, the country with the highest rate of suicide is the country of my birth. Regrettably, I have known too many that have died from this terrible scourge. I was lucky to survive my own attempts. My hope is that by applying scientific principles to this suicide phenomenon, I can shed some light on this subject and learn why Guyana in particular has the power to suck the life out of people who are broken. I hope to put forth some sort of antidote to this saddest of human conditions.

Further, it is my greatest hope that my experiences may in some way help others enduring similar circumstances in their life. One's starting point in life does not have to be the ending point in life. The human spirit does not have to be broken, or even if broken, it does not have to be beyond the point of repair. If we believe in a force greater than we are, we can know that all things are possible. Our species is remarkable in what it can endure and to what it can adapt. I hope that these words can serve as a message of hope, faith, endurance, and love to those who have been branded as unwanted, useless, incorrigible or defeated. Many might argue they do not have the strength to endure the sufferings of this world, but those thoughts could not be more wrong. God has given strength to all of us. No one is different from me; my story is real and I am enduring, so anyone else can as well. Just as I did, all it takes is to believe in a power stronger and wiser than any of us. With that belief will come the ability to move ahead one minute at a time, one hour at a time, one day at a time, one month at a time until ultimately it is possible to fulfill one's preordained purpose in life.

My relationship with God has blossomed to a level that I cannot quantify to anyone. I have closed my life to human intimate relationship and have now dedicated my life to serving God. I wonder if perhaps this is what He had always intended for me. I realize now that it is only people who disappoint and hurt each other whereas God Himself never does. I am forever grateful for the love and blessings that God has bestowed upon me and it is He who has given me everything meaningful in my life. I have lived a full life and have had countless experiences, both good and bad. Now, however, my remaining time in this life will be spent thanking God for my blessings and strengthening my relationship with Him in any way possible.

I pray that my children, also a blessing from God, will one day find their way back to me. If they do not, the love I have in my heart for them which many times I considered a curse, will be given to my fellow man. I once considered that love a curse because all it ever did was hurt me, but I have since grown to now recognize it as a blessing. A blessing that will joyfully be shared with mankind. Whatever I am blessed with or whatever trials or tribulations may come my way, I am sure of my steps because God has ordered them so. Although time continues to advance without any interaction with my children, and there being no expectation of seeing them any time soon, I trust in God and continue to hold on to my faith. They cannot know now how much I miss them, but the truth is here for them. Whether or not we are ever reunited, I know they too are in God's hands, the best hands possible.

Many have asked how I can maintain such faith and love in God through all these devastating life events. The answer is simple: He is God. The one who has created everything and ordered all existence. Although I may never understand why God allowed me to endure the tragedies in my life, I will forever believe in His judgment. Who am I to question his motives or decisions? One cannot simply love God when life is going well and then question or get angry at Him when it is not. Life is not about doing one's will. It is "His will be done." We are no wiser than God and we certainly do not know the end game. Only He does. So what one may perceive to be a bad thing, as in my wife's leaving, might very well turn out to be the greatest gift God has ever given. I say that with no malice. Through all my storms, and losing my family is without a doubt the most severe, I have never been closer to God and know Him the way I do now. Whatever becomes of me, I trust God. I thank my ex-wife for this beautiful gift as without her it would not have been possible to get to this point. As I step back and can begin to see a broader perspective, I have more faith and less fear.

I believe I now know what my purpose is and I am now actively seeking to fulfill that purpose. That purpose is to touch people's lives in some positive way and to encourage my fellow man to persevere even under the worst of circumstances. One is defeated only when one gives up. To forgive is what God wants of us, but never forget. We must use our experiences as a springboard for growth so, as painful as they may be, those experiences help me to remain grateful, grounded and faithful. I hold malice toward none, and I forgive all who have hurt me. I believe the following words to be true and will follow them to my last breath, "A new commandment I give to you, that you love one another, as I have loved you, that you also love one another."

ABOUT THE AUTHOR

As a teenage immigrant from Guyana to the United States, Robert Lawrie has lived the gamut of experiences. From living with an abusive father, to being homeless and being a victim of Church abuse, Robert has had to learn to manage life on his own. His various professional pursuits during his adult years as an entrepreneur gold miner and educator have also been laden with additional hardships and obstacles, including divorce, financial ruin and attempted suicide.

Despite the negative forces he has had to contend with, Rob maintains a positive outlook on life and has been able to survive as well as thrive. The compilation of his life experiences has driven Rob to share his life journey to help others see how they too can overcome the adversities they may face just as he done. He presently is a fourth year PhD student, a writer, an advocate for victims of abuse, for the disadvantaged and for education and is driven to inspire others to overcome.

To stay in touch with Rob and find out when his next book will be released, please visit his website at www. roblawrieauthor.com and sign up to receive occasional email notifications.